THE
GRAND
DESIGN

Male and Female He Made Them

OWEN STRACHAN
& GAVIN PEACOCK

D1494111

Confusion abounds today on what it means to be a man and what it means to be a woman. Peacock and Strachan put feet on the biblical teaching. God's word on what it means to be male and female isn't an abstraction. We are called upon to live out our calling as men and women in everyday life, and we can be grateful for Peacock's and Strachan's help in doing so.

TOM SCHREINER
James Buchanan Harrison Professor of New Testament Interpretation,
The Southern Baptist Theological Seminary, Louisville, Kentucky

Owen Strachan's writing renews the excitement and wonder of being alive. I'm so glad that he and Gavin Peacock have written this book. Our culture is desperate for men, for them to be Christ-like husbands and fathers. This book joins the great cause of meeting that need, and you'll be glad you read it.

JIM HAMILTON
Professor of Biblical Theology,
The Southern Baptist Theological Seminary, Louisville, Kentucky

Strachan and Peacock don't simply defend a view of men and women that is traditional but now counter-cultural. They show it is beautiful.

ANDY NASELLI
Assistant Professor of New Testament and Biblical Theology,
Bethlehem College & Seminary, Minneapolis, Minnesota

If you've ever driven in thick fog only to break out into clean, open air, you know the thrill of seeing vividly and clearly what before was hazy and confused. *The Grand Design* will do this for you on central matters of our human identity and experience as men and women, respectively. What riveting beauty and profound insight readers will find here, all with strong biblical fidelity. Some of the most pressing and difficult questions of our day related to human sexuality and gender are undertaken, and all for the purpose of depicting anew God's glorious design of manhood and womanhood. Read, rejoice, and realign through the fogless clarity of this book. It will change your life, and you'll give praise to God that it has.

BRUCE A. WARE
T. Rupert and Lucille Coleman Professor of Christian Theology,
The Southern Baptist Theological Seminary, Louisville, Kentucky

In an age so confused about identity and relationships between men and women, Strachan and Peacock have written an easily accessible and theologically clear must-read. Understanding our identity in Christ brings peace and fulfillment. Understanding the complementary relationships between men and women helps us glorifying God through the elegant dance of the sexes that point to the Gospel. This book will help with that and more as the reader gains personal understanding and the ability to help others who may be struggling.

Thomas White
President, Cedarville University, Cedarville, Ohio

Gender confusion permeates western society. Christians need a clear understanding of biblical teaching in this area, as a result. This book provides an emphatically complementarian exposition of Scripture's teaching on what it means to be man or woman, with particular focus on the home and the church. The authors are not afraid to confront and contradict secular consensus on the issues that arise. They have produced a challenging and practical volume which will repay careful study.

Robert Strivens
Principal, London Theological Seminary, London

We live in an age characterized by confusion on gender and sexuality. Christians need biblical wisdom and discernment in order to navigate our nation's sexual revolution. This short, clear, concise book from Owen Strachan and Gavin Peacock will help you live with fidelity in the midst of our cultural crisis. As this book demonstrates, the Bible's vision for gender complementarity is not only true but beautiful and good for the flourishing of marriages, families, and churches. Strachan and Peacock have provided a careful and faithful account of Scripture's vision for sexuality and gender. This book is urgently needed.

R. Albert Mohler, Jr.
President,
The Southern Baptist Theological Seminary, Louisville, Kentucky

The Grand Design won't be a popular book today but it is an enormously helpful and timely one. In the last chapter the authors state, 'The Bible is true. The Bible is good'. The rest of the book is a working out of that in relation to God's plan for men and women. In a subject where evangelicals are often defensive this book is relentlessly positive – seeking to extol God's glory in his wonderful design. In an area where evangelicals often say little beyond bland headlines, this book seeks to flesh out what manhood and womanhood actually look like. While you may not agree with every line, *The Grand Design* will encourage and empower you in living for God as the person God made you to be.

Nigel Beynon
Director of Word Alive, London

They've done it again. Owen Strachan, Gavin Peacock and the CBMW team have once again served the church in *The Grand Design*. In this short book they've laid out how biblical complementarity in the home and church is both good and glorious. I wish every Christian would read and apply *The Grand Design*.

Jason Allen
President, Midwestern Baptist Theological Seminary, Kansas City, Missouri

Gavin Peacock and Owen Strachan bring a compelling defence of God's design for masculinity and femininity by casting a beautiful vision of men and women as complementary expressions of the image of God. Their book is far more than readable and theologically rigorous. It is an inspiring manifesto for the church in the 21st century world.

Seemingly embarked on global conquest, contemporary Western individualism is doing all it can to undermine the family, promote a battle between the sexes and to blur the lines between genders. But Scripture informs us that every move to unravel God's patterns in Creation is actually an expression of his slow-motion judgement upon arrogant, blind and defiant humanity. This means that the so-called 'sexual revolution' has become an exercise in self-harm. Lost and confused, mankind needs rescuing and the church can only help as it brings the whole counsel of God to bear.

While many evangelicals compromise, or wear 'gospel only' blinkers, this book refuses to avoid any of the issues. With clarity, compassion and cultural awareness the authors have skilfully crafted a Biblical manual which will richly reward study and equip caring Christians to navigate contemporary society and reach out to our generation.

John Benton
Editor of Evangelicals Now &
Co-pastor of Chertsey Street Baptist Church, Guildford.

Men and Women today are still asking age old questions, but sadly are assuming or concluding there are no adequate answers. Muddled by the chaos and cacophony of the public square and a weakened teaching ministry of the churches, even those know instinctively where to find biblical True North, are stuttering when it comes to questions of manhood and womanhood. Finally, we have a right-sized book to answer the questions men and women are asking or need to ask. Gavin Peacock and Owen Strachan are skilled and gracious communicators and it is a joy to see *The Grand Design* in print. May it find its way into the hands of every man and woman on the planet.

Jason G. Duesing
Editor, The Journal for Biblical Manhood and Womanhood
Provost and Associate Professor of Historical Theology,
Midwestern Baptist Theological Seminary, Kansas City, Missouri

Confusion about gender roles is at the heart of so many problems today. This is true whether the issue concerns the cultural debates of homosexuality and transgender, public policy conflicts concerning women being drafted into combat, personal problems like fornication and pornography, church debates regarding women serving as pastors, or marital conflicts about who is in charge at home. We live among people who have lost their way on issues of manhood and womanhood. Owen Strachan and Gavin Peacock are reliable guides for the necessary return to biblical fidelity on one of our society's central confusions. Christian, you need to read this book.

HEATH LAMBERT
Executive Director, Association of Certified Biblical Counselors (ACBC);
Author, *A Theology of Biblical Counseling*

What a great and timely book on the issue of the role and function of men and women. Concise and biblical, it deals with everything from marriage, manhood, womanhood, transgender and, of course, homosexuality; all issues facing Bible believing Christians in our day. A very helpful primer for those of us who haven't really thought deeply about these topics and immensely practical for those of us facing serious questions on the coal face of Christian ministry and ethics.

MEZ MCCONNELL
Pastor, Niddrie Community Church and Ministry Director of 20Schemes

Few issues are more controversial in society and the church today that the Bible's teaching about men and women, gender roles and human sexuality. This is often misunderstood, misapplied or dismissed without careful consideration. Owen Strachan and Gavin Peacock have written a clear and compelling defence of God's design for men and women to be absolutely equal in status, but different in role. Rooted in careful exegesis they reveal the beauty of what God intends, and show how this has been tragically undermined in contemporary culture to the detriment of men and women. Whilst avoiding crass prescriptive stereotypes, they do no shy away from specific application of the biblical principles in marriage, the home, the workplace and the church, and they helpfully chart a Christian response to homosexuality and the rise of transgenderism. Above all they urge men and women to pursue godliness and submission to Christ in evert aspect of their lives, and to glorify him by embracing his good purposes for them. This book will encourage complementarians to be more confident in their convictions, and more faithful and loving in their practice, and will help egalitarians to understand complementarianism at its best.

JOHN STEVENS
National Director, Fellowship of Independent Evangelical Churches

The point of conflict in the cultural war, the place where the armies collide is clear. It is cosmic confusion over gender, sexual orientation, and sexual identity. In *The Grand Design* Peacock and Strachan have done the church an immense service. They have provided God's people with a valuable weapon, Truth! Read this little volume. It is a cup of cold water and in a dry and arid wasteland of lies and confusion.

WILLIAM FARLEY
Pastor and Author

Owen and Gavin have written a great book about one of the most present issues of our days; perhaps the most crucial issue in our generation: God's design for a man and a woman. It is about God, it is about God's wisdom and God's creation. But it is also about us… how are we to function complementing each other, as men and women in a beautiful and glorious way. God's design is for our own good and the authors will point that out to the reader. In addition, if you want to learn about why we cannot support the homosexual identity and the same sex marriage, this book is for you. It is thoroughly biblical, insightful, easy to read, courageous and challenging. Pick it up and read it! You will be glad you did it.

MIGUEL NÚÑEZ
Presidente, Ministerios Integridad y Sabiduría, Dominican Republic

God created man and woman in his own image, each with inherent dignity and worth and each with an equal share in the benefits of redemption through Christ. God has also assigned to man and woman different roles within the church and the home—roles that exemplify core gospel truths. These glorious realities point to the ultimate reality—Christ's self-sacrificial love for his bride. In *The Grand Design*, Owen Strachan and Gavin Peacock are calling us to see again the beauty of God's design for male and female. This is a timely and needed book.

DENNY BURK
Professor of Biblical Studies, Boyce College,
The Southern Baptist Theological Seminary, Louisville, Kentucky

The early church had concerns about Christology. The Reformers raised issues about soteriology. But today, we are faced with questions of anthropology. In an unprecedented way, there is confusion in the church about what it means to be created male and female. And so there has been a great need for a basic introduction to gender complementarity. *The Grand Design* fills this gap. For anyone beginning to search for answers to the epic questions of our age, Strachan and Peacock offer the way forward.

CLINT HUMFREY
Senior Pastor, Calvary Grace Church, Calgary, Alberta

THE
GRAND
DESIGN

Male and Female He Made Them

OWEN STRACHAN
& GAVIN PEACOCK

THE COUNCIL ON BIBLICAL
MANHOOD AND WOMANHOOD

CHRISTIAN
FOCUS

Owen Strachan is the President of the Council on Biblical Manhood & Womanhood. He is Associate Professor of Christian Theology and Director of the Center for Public Theology at Midwestern Baptist Theological Seminary in Kansas City, Missouri. The author or editor of thirteen books, he is married to Bethany and is the father of three children. He earned a PhD in Theological Studies from Trinity Evangelical Divinity School, an MDiv in Biblical & Theological Studies from Southern Seminary, and a BA in History from Bowdoin College.

Gavin Peacock is a husband to Amanda, father of Jake and Ava and a pastor at Calvary Grace Church in Calgary, Alberta. He is also CBMW's Director of International Outreach. He was a professional footballer for 18 years, and then worked for the BBC before entering full time ministry. He holds an MACS.

Scripture quotations are from *The Holy Bible, English Standard Version*, copyright © 2001 by Crossway Bibles, a publishing ministry of Good News Publishers. Used by permission. All rights reserved. ESV Text Edition: 2011.

paperback ISBN 978-1-78191-764-0
epub ISBN 978-1-78191-795-4
mobi ISBN 978-1-78191-796-1

10 9 8 7 6 5 4 3 2 1

Published in 2016
by
Christian Focus Publications Ltd,
Geanies House, Fearn, Ross-shire,
IV20 1TW, Great Britain.
www.christianfocus.com

Cover design by Paul Lewis

Printed by Bell & Bain, Glasgow

CONTENTS

Introduction

Paris. London. New York. Hong Kong. If you've ever had the chance to visit one of these remarkable cities, you know that the experience is far different than the preparation. Before you go, you surf the web, check out a few local restaurants near your hotel, and watch a video about an exciting attraction you'll see—a world-class museum, a theatre, a bookstore among them for many of us. But all the preparation does little to acclimate you to the breathless feeling you get when you're actually *there*, when you can smell, see, and hear a thriving metropolis in all its glory.

I (Owen) remember the first time I visited New York City. To walk through Central Park was a very different reality than glimpsing it in a film. To simply turn around 360 degrees and take the forest-turned-free-for-all in was nearly overwhelming. As I strolled around, I saw the effortless shaping of my surroundings. The park stretched before me and seemed to swallow me whole. The whole experience was deeply pleasant, and I'm eager to make this same discovery, to taste what you can only call serendipity, in other global cities.

This common experience relates to the theme of this book. Gavin and I tackle in these pages an introduction to biblical manhood and womanhood. Our subject is complementarity, the way in which men and women find happiness in owning their God-given identity and filling their God-given roles. Equal in dignity and worth, men and women share much in terms of Christian discipleship. But we are not the same. Unlike what egalitarianism would argue, men and women have different roles to play in life. We thus cannot agree with the idea that men and women alike lead in the home and church, as our egalitarian friends would say. The gospel of grace does not erase sexual difference and role distinctions; the gospel actually opens our eyes to savor divine design and our God-formed responsibilities.

The Lord has made us for His own pleasure, and He has given us unique form and calling. In the chapters that follow, we will show that the plan of God for men and women is not incidental, boring, or of glancing importance. It is a crucial part of Christian faith and practice. We think that what awaits you is much like what awaits a first-time traveler to Paris. You know some stuff about the City of Lights. You have a small sense of what this will be from past reading and browsing. You're happy to hear more and learn more, and you anticipate croissants and good coffee and lots of walking. For all your previous noodling, Paris in all its grandeur, all its beauty, is a discovery you can only make in person. It awaits you. It will intoxicate you. It will leave a mark on you, and you won't ever be the same.

This is true of biblical complementarity, as we will shortly see. We're not about to talk abstract pieties and numbing statistics. We're going to unfurl the beauty of God's creative work. We get a chance in this short book to savor the grand design of God. Many of us know that the creation is brimming with vitality and beauty. We can easily spot the smile of the Lord in the sea and the trees. But when it comes to our own bodies, to our own identities as men and women, the screen loses its color. The story fizzles. A gender-neutral world convinces us that manhood and womanhood aren't important. Complementarity is a fiction. It's no big deal to be a man or a woman.

Many people today believe secularism. They pursue androgyny. As a result, boys want to be girls today and girls want to be boys. Many men embrace the traits and attitudes traditionally associated with womanhood. Many women do the same with manhood. Both sides avoid at all costs hard-and-fast stereotypes. The ultimate transgression today is to fit into past conceptions of the sexes. Nobody wants to be some sort of manly man's mountain man or a Victorian-era tea-sipping countess. Men have grown increasingly passive, effeminate, and unsure of themselves. Women have grown increasingly manly, aggressive, and unsure of their future. These are hard words today, but they sum up the drift of a secularizing world.

In 2016, the sexes have lost the script for their lives, and so many of us don't know what role to play in life. Try asking a male friend at a coffee shop, 'What is your manhood *for*? What's the purpose of being a man?' Or try querying a young woman at the local university, 'What meaning does womanhood have? Does it matter at all?' A good number of folks would, in being asked these kind of questions, look at us like we had just invited them on a lunar cruise in a tugboat. Outside of affirming feminism, transgender identity, and shape-shifting sexual orientation, it's taboo today to speak of manhood and womanhood in any fixed way. This is true in secular circles, and it's increasingly true even in Christian circles.

This confusion extends to sex. When it comes to this perennial hot topic, we are told that fluidity trumps biology. There is no specific meaning of manhood and womanhood, and thus there is no structure or plan for sex. You just be who you choose to be, and you experiment with whoever strikes your fancy. You don't need to wait, you don't need to restrain your natural desires, you don't need to commit yourself. You need only to act on your impulses. When you're doing so, in fact, you find out who you truly are. You're then happy, alive, liberated, and *human*.

Christians have something better to offer—something impossibly better. We have an altogether different vision of human flourishing. The Scripture shows us that flourishing as a human means, ultimately, thriving as a man and a woman. This is a foundational truth of our existence, proceeding from pages 1 and 2 of the Bible. This means that coming to faith entails learning what manhood is and what womanhood is. It means we learn what our bodies are for, since learning about our bodies necessarily entails discovering who we are. God is no exotic gender theorist, separating anatomy from identity. As we shall see, the teaching of Scripture is that your body and your identity are bound, a whole, constituting a person, namely, *you*. Me.

The gospel unlocks these discoveries. When we trust Christ as our Savior, the beauty of God's design comes into view.

Our conversion opens our eyes to the nature and purpose of our God-given sex. We see the body not as a blunt instrument for our lusts, but as the gift of God for His glorification. We see our relationships with the opposite sex not as a power play, but as an opportunity to serve others in the name of Christ. We see the plan of complementarity, the roles we have the privilege of filling, not as a sentence to misery but as a summons to happiness. These discoveries come through the eyes of faith. We most savor the grand design when we know the great Designer.

For some readers, this big vision of the sexes may sound a bit odd. Is it really *that* big of a deal to be a man or woman? Sure, you may affirm the reality of two sexes, but aren't things less strict than they used to be? Maybe you wonder if the apostles who wrote the New Testament were simply men of their time, and so their exhortations and teachings matter less to us than first-century readers. Plus, we've all seen ways in which men and women both can overdo things. Some have grown up in genuinely restrictive environments and have been wounded by past instruction. Where this is the case, we grieve these abuses, which are no part of God's good will. Any perversion of biblical teaching owes not to the Word of God, but to the sinfulness of man, which unfortunately plays out all around us every day. It is not chauvinism or feminism that Scripture supports. God has something vastly better than what a broken, confused, predatory world offers us.

We're going to step in the Central Park of the universe in this book. Accustomed to disillusioning chaos and polluted streets, we're going to breathe fresh, clear air. We will see that all the Bible is pure, and reflects God's own mind. Neither jot nor tittle has passed away, Jesus said, which tells us that the Bible still instructs us in principle where it does not any longer instruct us in practice (Matt. 5:18).

This reflects the cherished words of Paul in 2 Timothy 3. 'All Scripture is breathed out by God,' the apostle informs us, 'and profitable for teaching, for reproof, for correction, and for training in righteousness, that the man of God may be complete, equipped for every good work' (2 Tim. 3:16-17). This means that all the written revelation of God has direct effect on our life, doctrine, and spirituality. We evangelicals may have been told that some parts of the Scripture are really important, some are kind-of important, and some you can take or leave. But as we'll show in the pages to come, this ranking system will not do.

Yes, some doctrines reside at the burning core of living faith. You must believe them to know God. Salvation hinges on them. No, not every matter in the Bible is equally easy to parse out (eschatology, for one). Yes, we have charity toward younger Christians who may not know all their theological niceties. No, there is not complete agreement among complementarians (those who hold, at base, to male leadership and feminine submission in the home and church) on all the outworkings of scriptural teaching.

Get ready, friends. We want to do something radical in our time: we want to celebrate God's Word. We want to savor a crucial part of the whole counsel of God. After all, we are not the too-cool-for-school postmodern cynic who deigns to assent to the parts of Scripture that strike his fancy (and that sound good to his non-Christian friends). We are the Psalmist, exclaiming, 'Oh, how I love your law!'

We're not in this for condemnation. We're in this for exaltation. We're in this for delight. We want to see men and women captured by the gospel come alive to the beauty of manhood and womanhood. We want to see marriages roar to life, children well-taught and well-loved, singles filled with hope, churches pulsing with happy holiness, and societies influenced by gracious and convictional complementarian witness.

We know that this is a big vision and a big goal. But we worship a big God and trust a great gospel. It is a gospel so great that it takes ruined, messed-up, confused people and turns them into living doxology. We are called to a way of life that shows that Jesus is more than fire insurance. The faith is a worldview, an embodied worldview. When we trust Christ, we inherit a new way of seeing. We are like new arrivals to a thrilling city. It's fun to look at a street map or a café website. But we are those who see not only the details, the raw data of a new and better place, but the grand design of it all.

To that spectacular design we now turn.

CHAPTER ONE

What Is Biblical Complementarity?

Twenty-two years after scoring against Manchester United, now and then I (Gavin) will watch that goal and hear the commentator on the video.

> 'Clarke with the shot.
> It's off the keeper's hands…
> Peacock driving in…
> GOAL!
> Chelsea take the lead!'

More than that I can still feel the electricity and euphoria of the moment. It was the kind of moment every boy in England dreams of. Playing for Chelsea, I saw the shot from 20 yards out by my teammate, Steve Clarke. I instinctively tore in toward the goal at full-speed, ready for the rebound off the keeper, and found the back of the net. With that, we took the lead over Manchester United, a lead we never relinquished. We beat them 1-0 at home and away that season and I scored the winning goal each time: a rare feat against the best team in the country.

It was a dream to play against David Beckham, Ryan Giggs, and several of the world's greatest athletes. People looked at you as a star, a man's man, the one who had achieved the dreams of the many. Whether basketball, football, baseball, or other sports, countless children all over the world dream of just the kind of experience I was blessed to have with teams like Chelsea, Newcastle and QPR over eighteen years and 600 games as a professional.

But here's what I knew then, and know now: being an accomplished footballer isn't what brings happiness in this world. More than that, success in sports—or business, Hollywood, politics, law—isn't what makes you a man. Here we come face to face with a major problem, though: many boys have no idea today what it means to be a man.

This is every bit as true for women as it is for men. With my coauthor, Owen, I know the hopes and fears of men in a directly personal way. But I know that women are just as tempted to define who they are by worldly, non-biblical standards. If many boys yearn to be an athlete, a heroic celebrity who gets all the fame and money, many little girls grow up wanting to be beautiful. They want to be liked and attractive. They are encouraged to be strong today, to assert themselves over boys and show that they're better. Many girls have been trained to think they know what womanhood is, but the truth is, they're just as confused as many boys are.

Today, the sexes seem to be in a zero-sum competition. This means that one side wins and the other loses. There is no togetherness, no teamwork. Either men rule the world or women do. In the age of progress, the sexes are more divided than ever before.

To understand manhood and womanhood, and to heal the divide between the sexes, you have to go to a different source than the newscasters and highlights. You have to close the magazines and fansites. You have to ignore the celebrity rags and entertainment shows. To understand what it means to be a man or a woman, and to begin to appreciate the grand design of God for humanity, you have to go to the Bible.

So that's where we now turn.

Mankind as the Image of God

The Bible announces something truly radical in its first chapter, Genesis 1. It depicts mankind as the direct creation of Almighty God. Mankind is no genetic accident. On the sixth day of creation, after the Lord has formed the heavenly bodies, the earth, the birds and beasts, and much more, He makes Adam. This is His last creative stroke, and His timing signals that this is His masterwork.

In making the man, God communicates His intent for humanity. He wants the human race to function as His living image, as Genesis 1:26 makes clear:

> Then God said, 'Let us make man in our image, after our likeness. And let them have dominion over the fish of the sea and over the birds of the heavens and over the livestock and over all the earth and over every creeping thing that creeps on the earth.'

Adam alone is made in the image of God. Parrots, fruit trees, and comets all testify to the glory of God, but none are the image of God. Only mankind physically represents the Lord. Only mankind rules over the rest of creation. With all due apologies to salamanders and salmon, God has not made fish king over other beings. It is mankind that rules, and that is to 'take dominion' of the God-made world.

This passage reveals that mankind is the representation of God on earth. There is incredible nobility and dignity in this identity. It is not only the most impressive human specimens who carry this title, *Image of God*. It is every single person, boy and girl, man and woman. We are united in this glorious truth. When you are looking at a person, you are seeing a little picture, however insufficient, of God Himself.

Genesis 1 teaches us a second vital truth: an essential part of being an image-bearer is maleness and femaleness. Genesis 1:27 speaks to this aspect of our human identity:

> *So God created man in his own image,*
> *in the image of God he created him;*
> *male and female he created them.*

This poetic verse underscores what we have just covered. Three times in the Bible's first chapter mankind is called the 'image' of God, which shows us that God is signaling to us to not miss this teaching. Adam, the first human, is specially identified as the man who first images God. But Adam is not to be alone, roaming over the earth on the back of a triceratops. This God-designed realm features both 'male and female.' The language of this concept is loaded with intentionality: *He created* male and female.

God, the Bible is telling us, did this. He made men and women. He designed their form and frame. He programmed their biology and physiology. Man as male and female does not owe to an evolutionary outworking, but to divine intent. When you look at a man, you are supposed to think, *God designed that structure—amazing!* When you look at a woman, you are supposed to think, *God's own mind created her—incredible!*

We need to quickly consider a matter that readers sometimes stumble over. The fact that both men and women bear the image of God doesn't mean that God is both male and female. He is exclusively identified in Scripture in masculine terms, though He is a spirit and does not have a physical body (Jesus did and does, obviously, and He was a man).[1] We must address God the Father as God the Son instructed us to address Him: 'Our Father,' we learn to pray in Matthew 6:9. This is not a matter of preference, it is a matter of obedience to our Maker. The name of God speaks to the character of God.[2] We do not call God whatever we like; while we love various metaphors for God from Scripture, we address Him as God Himself has instructed us.

We need to mark this: while God designed humanity for relationship, each person *is* the image of God. The

---

1. To better understand the implications of the manhood of Christ, see Bruce Ware, *The Man Christ Jesus: Theological Reflections on the Humanity of Christ* (Wheaton, IL: Crossway, 2012).

2. For guidance on this tricky question, see Bruce A. Ware, 'How Shall We Think About the Trinity,' in *God Under Fire: Modern Scholarship Reinvents God*, ed. Douglas S. Huffman and Eric L. Johnson (Grand Rapids: Zondervan, 2009), 253-78. One quotation suffices here: '[T]he Bible never employs feminine metaphorical language to name God. True, God is sometimes said to be or to act in ways like a mother (or some other feminine image), but never is God called "Mother" as he is often called "Father." Respect for God's self-portrayal in Scripture requires that we respect this distinction. While we have every right (and responsibility) to employ feminine images of God, as is done often in Scripture itself, no biblical example or precedence would lead us to go further and to name God in ways he has not named himself' (266-67).

fact that male and female alike image God does not mean that each is 50% of the image. God desires both sexes to display His intelligence, relational nature, instinct for dominion, and more. Both men and women possess traits that mirror God's own person. The Lord has programmed all humanity, including both men and women, to serve as a living embodiment of His glory. God, nonetheless, identifies Himself in exclusively male terms in Scripture, and so must we when we speak of Him and pray to Him. His self-identification in masculine terms—Father—tells us something crucial about His own identity and also the creation order.

Our maleness and femaleness are so basic we sometimes take these realities for granted. But this is the wrong response. There is doxology in the details. We should glory in manhood and womanhood. We should see them as the Scripture sees them: the successful enfleshment of the Creator's super-intelligent plan for humanity. God made these forms, and God made these persons. God clearly loves diversity. He desires to see the distinct beauty displayed in the unique frames and make-ups of the sexes.

But God wasn't making museum pieces. He is at His core an acting God, and He had plans for men and women. Genesis 1:28 spells out the plan in brief:

> And God blessed them. And God said to them, 'Be fruitful and multiply and fill the earth and subdue it, and have dominion over the fish of the sea and over the birds of the heavens and over every living thing that moves on the earth.'

The first humans had duties. They were to do several things, according to the Lord:

1) Be fruitful and multiply
2) Fill the earth and subdue it
3) Have dominion over all things

The first duty was a direct call to procreation. The first couple was to come together in sexual union as one man and one woman to produce children. God designed sex for the man and the woman and their offspring to enjoy. He wanted them to bear fruit, essentially, language that suggests viewing pregnancy and subsequent childbirth as a joyous event. God wanted His image to spread over all the earth through marital sex.

The man and the woman were further called to 'subdue' and 'take dominion' over the earth. They ruled over the created order, which needed stewardship and shaping. Even before the fall, the first couple needed to work with their world to arrange it for God's praise. Thus we see that mankind had marching orders from the start. They had work on the to-do list, none of it cursed, all of it delightful.[3]

Adam and Eve were supposed to populate the world while ruling over the creation. God was their king; they, in turn, walked the earth as vice-king and vice-queen. As Genesis 2 shows, they worked in unity, but they filled different roles. Their bodies were complementary; their God-given roles were complementary.

Every word in Genesis 1 is crucial for understanding human identity. Here, these four words bear great weight: *And God blessed them.* The Lord gave both man and woman His special favor. All His creation carried the smell and look

---

3. For an enlightening take on what our humanity enables us to positively tackle in this God-made world, see Joe Rigney, *The Things of Earth: Treasuring God by Enjoying His Gifts* (Wheaton, IL: Crossway, 2014).

of a divinely-designed world. Everywhere one looked, one saw an order teeming with life, heard happy sounds, smelled the scent of a harmonious place. Nothing was fallen; nothing was wrong.

All the world was happy, and the first couple—Adam and Eve according to Genesis 2—was especially happy. God loved them specially. He looked on them with special love. He was not a super-contractor meeting someone else's design specifications. God was, and is, a Father. At the height of His creative work, on the sixth day, He became a Father. He looked on His children with unwavering delight. *And God blessed them.* The world hummed with the Father's good grace.

Here we pause to unpack the word used in the chapter title: *complementarity.* The sexes are complementary—that is, they are different but fit together. The man and the woman did not have the same form; their bodies were designed with notable differences. But they were not so different as to be unworkable. God made these distinct physiques so that the man and woman could join together in sexual union.[4]

Christian theologians and pastors often use complex language when talking about marriage and sex. But there is nothing formal or sober about God's call to be fruitful and multiply. The opportunity to join Adam and Eve in fulfilling what is called the 'dominion mandate' is a wondrous one. The happiness and satisfaction and togetherness offered to us in marital sex are remarkable. Only a divine mind could design it.

---

4. The standard reference work on biblical complementarity is the magisterial text by Wayne Grudem and John Piper, *Recovering Biblical Manhood and Womanhood* (Wheaton, IL: Crossway, 2012 [1991]). *RBMW* expresses the basic commitments of the international complementarian movement, the nerve center of which is the Council on Biblical Manhood & Womanhood (CBMW). Access the CBMW website at http://www.cbmw.org.

If that's not enough, we're offered in sex something much more than just a powerful experience. Sex has consequences, very good ones: it produces children. It allows mankind to taste the inexpressible joy of creating life, stewarding life, and building something bigger than oneself. We have been trained to think of the results of sex—children—as a negative, when in truth they are God-ordained and deeply fulfilling. Life-making is life-giving.

Sex will not give us ultimate happiness. It was never intended to do so, and it never will, much as the latest round of pop songs say otherwise. Sex is a gift, and a functional gift. It will not complete us, renew us, and it certainly will not save us. It was not made to be worshipped, but to be enjoyed according to the plan of God. Christians are able with many people to be thankful for sex, but we see that sex has a particular order—one man and one woman united in marriage—and a particular goal—the glory of God through honoring the plan of God. All this can happen only when complementarity is practiced and celebrated. The sexes were not made for competition; they were made for one another.

The structure and symmetry of the God-made world take your breath away.

To Work and to Help: Male and Female Identity

Genesis 2 fills out the groundwork laid by Genesis 1. It zeroes in on the Lord's formation of the man and woman. Adam, we learn, was made 'from the dust of the ground,' and air first filled his lungs when 'the Lord breathed into his nostrils the breath of life' (Gen. 2:7). We cannot help but see here the special care God took to make and care for Adam.

The intimacy of this act of creation is striking. The Lord formed Adam like a sculptural masterpiece, and lit the spark of life in His creation by breathing into him. The care, tenderness, and intentionality of God's work take our breath away. So far from a chance act, a design-free evolutionary jump, Adam's life owes only—and directly—to God's intervention. He is a creature from the start, wholly dependent on God, able to live and move and have his being solely because of God.

The Lord placed Adam in Eden 'to work it and keep it' (Gen. 2:15). We are not reading stage directions in these verses. We are getting vital information about Yahweh's intention for the first man. Adam is called from the very start of his life to work. He is given responsibility beneath the sovereignty of God, responsibility that has massive implications. There is a great teeming garden to tend and cultivate. Adam's duties have great import, and the Lord has honored His creation with this commission. A man, reading this passage, is to feel excitement and joy at the privilege of joining Adam—even as Adam joined God—in being a worker.

God grants tremendous trust to the man. He gives him a powerful charge, telling him he must not eat of the fruit of the tree of the knowledge of good and evil (2:17). Doing so will bring death. This is a sign to Adam that he has conditions to meet even in Eden. He must obey the Lord, and keep His charge, His covenant, or else suffer the consequences of disobedience. Yahweh also signals that Adam is lacking one thing: a 'helper,' an *ezer* in Hebrew, a word used for many Old Testament figures, including God Himself. The fact that Adam is 'alone' is 'not good' to the Lord, a striking statement (2:18). Again, Eden is not heaven. It is a place infused with the glory and favor of God, but it is not perfected. Adam needs a wife.[5]

---

5. Read more about the beauty of marriage in John Piper, *This Momentary Marriage: A Parable of Permanence* (Wheaton, IL: Crossway, 2009).

Here the concept of 'complementarity' really clicks into place. Adam, like the vast majority of men, was not made to walk alone throughout life. He needed a woman 'fit for him,' suited to him. This means that the helper needed to be *like him* as a human (and not a beast or flower) but *distinct from him*. This is the essence of complementarity: one suited to us, who fits with us, but is not precisely the same as us.

We do not live in an age that celebrates the distinctiveness of the sexes. Encountering a statistic about male-female distinctiveness is increasingly like meeting a killer whale on a London street: it doesn't happen. We should note that we don't ground our views on complementarity in any laboratory or scientific study. But we're glad to find truth wherever we can, knowing that God is the author of it, and this world is filled with reasonable conclusions and principles that point to Him.

It may surprise readers to know that men, on average, have over 1,000 per cent more testosterone coursing through their body than women. Whenever I speak at a conference or church on the subject, I ask people to raise their hands if they've heard that data point. Almost no one does. The gender-neutralizing, distinctive-denying culture doesn't wish to share such matters.[6] But we need to know these life-shaping facts. UK authors Bill and Anne Moir explain the significance of differing testosterone levels:

---

6. For the perspective of a feminist scholar who advocates the 'social construc-tivist' view of gender like Judith Butler, *Gender Trouble and the Subversion of Identity* (London: Routledge, 1990). This view leans upon the idea that societies 'construct' a standard view of the sexes, but that these constructions owe to myth, not reality. The view put forth in this chapter and promoted by Scripture is often called 'gender essentialism,' namely, that the sexes are different in meaningful ways.

Men's competitive drive comes from testosterone, and, because in real life not everyone can be a winner, it will come as no surprise that testosterone levels vary between individuals. They also vary enormously between men and women: the adult male's T levels (5,140-6,460 units) are about eleven times higher than a woman's (285-440 units). Give a man the challenge of competition and his already high T level will rise, increasing still further his competitive edge.[7]

The Moirs note that these findings may unsettle modern readers: 'Life is not fair.' They continue by noting that both sexes profit from their distinctive bodies: 'A man can jog away the pounds, but a woman cannot. She has to diet too.' This is true, according to the Moirs, of those who compete in track-and-field. In such events, 'males have a 10 per cent advantage, and nature will keep it that way.' The average man, at base, 'can burn energy faster than she can. Not only that, but women carry a higher proportion of body fat than men because women are more efficient at converting energy into storage.' Because of this, 'She might survive famine, but he will always run faster.'[8]

The point seems obvious enough, though it is considered 'controversial' today. Men and women are physically different. Men on average can lift more weight than women, run faster than women, and perform markedly better in combat situations. If the Moirs are correct in the foregoing, these basic

---

7. Anne and Bill Moir, *Why Men Don't Iron: The Fascinating and Unalterable Differences Between Men and Women* (New York: Citadel Press, 1999), 56. See also Michael Gurian, *The Wonder of Boys* (New York: Tarcher, 2006).

8. Anne and Bill Moir, *Why Men Don't Iron*, 165-66.

physiological realities suggest that men and women are not the same. As Catholic theologian John Paul II put it, the sexes are 'different even in the deepest bio-physiological determinants.'[9]

The differences between the sexes should factor into the big and small decisions we all make. This includes, quite crucially, parents. But because of a difference-averse culture, fewer and fewer parents think about such matters in our time, though. I saw a surprising example of this play out in public not too long ago. A journalist named Michael Sokolove bravely sounded the horn in the *New York Times* about the huge disparity in injuries between boys and girls who play contact sports. Sokolove is not an evangelical, and he has his own perspective on these matters. Nevertheless, he noted the following: 'If girls and young women ruptured their Anterior Cruciate Ligaments at just twice the rate of boys and young men, it would be notable. Three times the rate would be astounding.' He concluded the point: '[F]emale athletes rupture their A.C.L.s at rates as high as five times that of males.'[10]

---

9. John Paul II, *Man and Woman He Created Them: A Theology of the Body* (Pauline Books & Media, 2006), 211. Though we are not Catholic, we deeply appreciate this insightful word from the same section: 'The theology of the body contained in Genesis is concise and sparing with words. At the same time, fundamental and in some sense primary and definitive contents find expression in it. All human beings find themselves in their own way in that biblical "knowledge." Woman's constitution differs from that of man; in fact, we know today that it is different even in the deepest bio-physiological determinants. The difference is shown only in a limited measure on the outside, in the build and form of her body. Motherhood shows this constitution from within, as a particular power of the feminine organism, which serves with creative specificity for the conception and generation of human beings with the concurrence of the man. "Knowledge" conditions begetting.'

10. Michael Sokolove, 'The Uneven Playing Field,' *New York Times* magazine, May 11, 2008. See also Sokolove, *Warrior Girls: Protecting Our Daughters Against the Injury Epidemic in Women's Sports* (New York: Simon &

This is a staggering finding. One would think that Sokolove would receive applause for pointing it out. No doubt some appreciated it, but the journalist's writing drew ferocious pushback. One article by Steven D. Stovitz and Elizabeth A. Arendt suggested that Sokolove's writing should be written off simply for suggesting that the sexes are not the same: 'One major theme [of his piece] is that females simply can't do what males do. Therefore, when they try to "act like males," meaning be competitive, powerful and aggressive, they will inevitably become injured.'

Sokolove, whose article was by no means detrimental to women, was guilty in the eyes of Stovitz and Arendt (and many others) of 'overwrought language' which 'contributes to the sense of fear he creates when discussing the "injury epidemic" he claims exists.'[11] The reason for higher injury rates was unknowable, claimed Stovitz and Arendt. They simply wrote off essential bodily differences, despite the fact that such differences are plain as day and require no medical training to intuitively grasp.

We share this strange exchange for one reason: it illustrates the confusion of our culture over the sexes. We have effectively blinded ourselves to physical differences, which is to say the core realities of manhood and womanhood. This does not mean, of course, that there are not women who are far better athletically than men, or women and men alike whose bodily experience counters the norm. In addition, no one is justified in concluding that women are physically

---

Schuster, 2008).

11. Steven D. Stovitz and Elizabeth A. Arendt, 'Anatomy Isn't Destiny: A Response to Michael Sokolove (A Sports Medicine Perspective),' *The Tucker Center Newsletter*, Fall 2008. Accessed online at http://www.cehd. umn.edu/tuckercenter/newsletter/2008-fall/feature.htm.

inferior to men. The design of God for men and women is intentional, and no value difference should be seen in bodily difference.

The differences between the sexes matter. They matter quite significantly. We must honor them to understand ourselves, to understand complementarity, and to thrive as men and women, husbands and wives. Complementarity is the fabric of marriage, and is the guarantor of the survival of the human race. Without complementarity (of a sexual kind), children will not exist. In this sense, we are all complementarians—at least anyone who wants to have a child is. Even scientists in a laboratory must honor complementarity to produce life in a petri dish.

This discussion helps us understand how the Lord views women. Some people might read the preceding material and think: *That shows us that the Bible is anti-woman. It demeans women by calling them a helper, after all. Women are relegated to doing nothing but wringing out hand-towels and picking lint off their aprons!* We understand this objection, and we recognize that our secular culture only encourages it. But for people who love the Word of God, this response will not suffice.

For starters, it does not do justice to the creative intention of God. God has not suggested by His designation that women are extraneous and unimportant. On the contrary, He has suggested that women are absolutely needful. It's *not good* that Adam has no helper. He needs someone to fill that role. She will bring strengths, gifts, abilities, and proclivities that he will benefit from, and that only she possesses. Adam can't fill this role. It's not that he's crying in the corner; he can *function* without a wife. But without Eve, his existence will be impoverished, and God's plan of dominion will lie slack. The biblical text makes clear that his life is missing blessings God wants him to have, blessings that Adam himself cannot produce.[12]

Biblical womanhood is the most exciting take on femininity the world has ever seen. Genesis 2 suggests that a woman has inherent value as the special creation of the Lord. Women do not need to be beautiful, attractive, omnicompetent, outgoing, or powerful to have value. Already, as God-created women, they have value. They possess dignity. Almighty God has spoken to the nature of womanhood, and He has shown that He sees it as essential for human flourishing.

There is simply no place in biblical Christianity for a diminished view of womanhood. The role given to the woman—*helper*—signifies that she will fill a vital role, and apply unique gifts, to the world God has made. This identity comes in the context of marriage, but it speaks to the nature of womanhood even beyond the marital relationship. Being a helper applies first to covenantal union, but this core trait does not shut off—or only activate—on the day of a wedding. Godly women train their daughters to own this attribute from their earliest days, seeing in Genesis 2 a sign of who God made them to be.

We see that the sexes are not designed for competition. They are made for cooperation. Their purposes are intertwined. God literally made one sex for the other, the woman for the man. This last reality may stretch things for some readers, but it is biblically indisputable. Think of 1 Corinthians 11, where Paul builds on Genesis 1 and 2: 'For man was not made from woman, but woman from man. Neither was man created for

---

12. For more on the beauty of a godly wife and mother, see Carolyn Mahaney, *Feminine Appeal: Seven Virtues of a Godly Wife and Mother* (Wheaton, IL: Crossway, 2012).

woman, but woman for man' (1 Cor. 11:8-9). If this seems offensive, we do well to remember that the Bible shapes our thinking, not the culture. God ordered the sexes by creating them according to His own plan. We have no authority to deny this plan or demote it. It is a good plan, and a good order.

So far from domination, there is an interdependence between the first couple that is missing from our modern understanding of the sexes. Men are not made to be lone warriors, isolated and estranged from women. Women are not made to divest themselves from men, sneering at any thought of connection. For most people, the interdependence of marriage is not only good, but crucial. [13]

Blissful complementarity, not biting conflict, is God's intention.

The Glory of Marital Union

We have seen already that the Lord called Adam to work and to lead in His creation. Shortly after this call, we see Adam acting in this role, naming the animals and birds as God brought them before him (Gen. 2:19). Here again we marvel at the Lord's investment of trust in Adam. The Lord, a loving father, sought to raise up a righteous son by giving him responsibility and meaningful labor. Adam did so, and no doubt experienced profound satisfaction in his God-given role.

Then the portrait of the early days of creation becomes ethereal. Adam drops into a deep sleep by the design of God (Gen. 2:21). The Lord takes a rib from his body and forms the woman from the man (Gen. 2:21-22). Here again we

---

13. To understand the practical import of this reality, see Darrin Patrick, *The Dude's Guide to Marriage: Ten Skills Every Husband Must Develop to Love His Wife Well* (Nashville, TN: Thomas Nelson, 2015).

are in strange and wondrous territory. The Lord personally performs this act of creation, making Eve by His own hand just as He made Adam. Yahweh is a craftsman.[14]

We cannot miss the significance of the woman's formation. She came into being through Adam's own body. Without his losing a rib, she would not have existed. The implications of this truth are profound. Every time Adam looked at Eve, he would think, 'She came from my body!' Every time Eve looked at Adam, she would think, 'He gave his body for me!' Yahweh communicated something impossibly profound in this physiological feat. The man is summoned by God to revere and protect the woman; the woman is summoned by God to respect and trust the man. This is the strongest argument in all the earth against masculine abuse and feminine distrust. Love is coded into the very body of the first man and the first woman.

Both spouses have entered into a relationship that is straightforwardly bodily—he a man, she a woman—but mystical.[15] This is physical complementarity in action, but more is happening in this union. Their destinies are intertwined; they have unique features and traits; they are being knit together in a strange and wondrous dance. We are used to hearing about the wonders of science today, often from a non-Christian standpoint. Let it be shouted from the rooftops that there is nothing more awe-inducing in all the

---

14. For a richly detailed study of manhood and womanhood, see Andreas Köstenberger and Margaret Elizabeth Köstenberger, *God's Design for Man and Woman: A Biblical-Theological Survey* (Wheaton, IL: Crossway, 2014).

15. For more on the ethereal nature of marital union, see Mike Mason, *The Mystery of Marriage: Meditations on the Miracle* (Colorado Springs: Multnomah, 2005).

natural order than this, the man and the woman united in purpose and love.

Adam shouts with joy when he sets eyes on his wife. He is not indifferent or distracted. As seen in Genesis 2:23, he is overjoyed at what God has wrought:

> *This at last is bone of my bones*
> *and flesh of my flesh;*
> *she shall be called Woman,*
> *because she was taken out of Man.*

Oftentimes, these words are read soberly in Christian settings. In truth, they deserve to be shouted at full volume! We suspect that is how Adam, his eyes alight, gave voice to them.

At the close of Genesis 2, the narrator breaks in, and tells us what this scene means for the rest of humanity. The blueprint for the forming of a family is simple, but as we have seen, majesty and beauty are woven into this design: 'Therefore a man shall leave his father and his mother and hold fast to his wife, and they shall become one flesh. And the man and his wife were both naked and were not ashamed' (Gen. 2:24-25). This is the plan of God for the filling of the earth and the enactment of human dominion over the created realm. A man takes leadership to begin a family by leaving his father and mother. He finds a wife and 'holds fast' to her. He never lets her go, never relinquishes his protection of her, never abandons her and his children. He looks her in the eye and tells her, 'I will never leave you. I am never walking out on you and our children. Never.'

For her part, the woman will soon become 'mother of all living' (Gen. 3:20). She was made for this. The Protestant Reformer Martin Luther made plain why this is so: '[B]y nature woman has been created for the purpose of bearing children. Therefore she has breasts; she has arms for the purpose of nourishing, cherishing, and carrying her offspring. It was the intention of the Creator that women should bear children and that men should beget them.'[16] Eve was made for 'one-flesh' union with Adam. Their intimacy will make Adam a father and Eve a mother. This is the holy design of God. Marriage brings delight, as the couple channel their God-given sexual passion to one another, and by divine aid produce children.

Today, we are tempted to see extramarital 'hookups' as normal and marital affection as somehow weird and untoward. The opposite is true. There is nothing more normal and natural than one man and one woman united in marriage. This is the plan of God for most people. In describing these things, we are on holy ground.

It All Falls Down: Gender Roles After Sin

The air of Genesis 2 is so fresh and pure, innocent and calming. The air of Genesis 3 seems polluted by comparison. As recorded in Genesis 3:1-7, sin enters the world. It does so by instigation of Satan, who takes on the identity of a serpent and urges Adam and Eve to eat the forbidden fruit from the tree of the knowledge of good and evil. Though we sometimes think of God and Satan in the abstract, in the early chapters of Genesis both speak directly to the man and woman. The Bible's first chapters introduce us to the vivid conflict playing out between God and the devil—with the fate of mankind hanging in the balance.

---

16. Martin Luther, *Luther's Works* (St. Louis: Concordia Publishing House, 1955-present), 5:355.

Adam should have protected his wife, rebuked the serpent, and exercised his God-given dominion over a beast that creeps on the ground. He was given this powerful role in Genesis 1. But he does no such thing. He hides instead of leading and protecting his wife. As a result, the beast takes dominion of mankind, and then Eve leads Adam. The order of creation instituted by God is reversed, and the man and woman sin against the Lord, and death enters the world.

The Lord will not tolerate this inversion of authority, however. When He visits the man and woman after their sin, He addresses the man: 'Where are you?' (Gen. 3:9). The 'you' is singular in the Hebrew, and Adam instantly—though no doubt reluctantly—responds. He blames the woman for his sin: 'The woman you gave me' provided food for him (Gen. 3:12). Actually, Adam blames both the woman *and* God Himself in this terrible response. Here is the first historical instance of masculine blame-shifting, of men not taking responsibility for the evil they have allowed to enter their homes.[17]

The Lord pronounces sentence upon the serpent and the couple in Genesis 3:15-19. He promises that the serpent's head will be crushed, indicating that a redeemer will come to undo the death-work of Satan. He tells Eve that she will have pain in childbearing and that her husband will rule over her, indicating that this rule will be difficult for her due to his sin. He tells Adam that he will work the ground in pain and sweat, and this because he listened to the voice of his wife.

The curse is a curse upon existing complementarian roles. The woman does not become a childbearer in the curse; Adam does not become a worker after the fall. The curse falls upon

---

17. To understand how a man can rebel against his natural sinful instincts and instead become a leader, consult Steve Farrar, *Point Man: How a Man Can Lead His Family* (Colorado Spring, CO: Multnomah Books, 2003).

the pre-fall, God-created roles of men and women. Even after the fall, the man and woman function as God intended them, producing a child, clothed despite their nakedness in animal skins (Gen. 3:21). The Lord has covered His people in robes that foreshadow the justifying righteousness of Christ. The curse is effectual, but it is not ultimately triumphant.

As Genesis 3 closes, the good design of God has taken a massive hit, but the complementarity of the sexes still stands, and still promises tremendous blessing to all who will receive it as good. Nothing can undo the will of God.

The Rest of the Story

The complementarity of the sexes is based in the monumental first chapters of Scripture. This is why we have worked through this portion of the Bible with care. To understand God's design for men and women, you cannot simply jump to the New Testament. You must understand what God originally desired and decreed for the sexes as laid out in Genesis 1-3. Only then will you know the intent of divine design. The sexes come from God's own mind, image God's own glory, and fulfill God's own plan. This is vital, not optional, material. Without it, we simply cannot understand what follows.

We have much more to study about men and women in the chapters to come. For now, we should mark several ways that the New Testament upholds and expands upon the material thus far studied.

—In Matthew 19:3-6, Jesus upholds the original design of God for marriage in His comments on divorce, defining marriage as the union of one man and one woman for life. Jesus affirms not simply the plan of God for marriage, but the basic identity of the sexes. In His mind, they are distinct but suited for union.

—In Ephesians 5:22-33, Paul teaches that marriage images the salvific relationship between Christ and His church. He calls husbands to love their wives and wives to submit to their husbands as unto the Lord. This material fills out what Ephesians 5:21 calls for: appropriate subjection to proper authorities. It is to be read in line with Ephesians 6:1-4, where Paul calls for children to be subject to their parents.

—In 1 Corinthians 11:1-16, Paul teaches that women are the glory of men, indicating the proper order of creation, one spelled out in Genesis 2. Paul also charges the church to honor the distinct design of the sexes. He wants women to dress and look like women, and men to dress and look like men. This corroborates Deuteronomy 22:5, which forbids cross-dressing.

—In 1 Timothy 2:9-15, Paul calls for men to serve as elders and teachers in the church (see also 1 Tim. 3:1-7; Titus 1:5-9). He grounds this call in the order of creation, noting that men have a God-given responsibility to lead. This duty of teaching and exercising elder-like leadership among God's people applies broadly, as fits the context. It is not an office that Paul calls men to hold; in other words, it is a function that he charges men to exercise. This consists of leading and teaching the people of God. This is the exclusive call of men.

—In 1 Peter 3:1-7, Peter calls for wives to submit to their husbands, following them with a joyful, respectful posture. He delineates a womanly spirit from a man's, marking it as 'gentle and quiet' (1 Pet. 3:4). He calls for men to live with their wives in an understanding way, ruling out a posture of lordly unkindness in husbands.

This sampling of several key features of New Testament complementarity shows that they build upon the Old Testament's sound foundation. The focus of coming chapters will center in the New Testament's teaching on manhood, womanhood, marriage, and church life, allowing us to flesh out the preceding section in much greater detail. All told, we will see that the Bible speaks with one voice to the beauty of complementarity.

The Scripture holds fast to the original teaching of Genesis. It does not begin with a careful delineation of manhood and womanhood, each grounded in the concept of image-bearing, and then shed this moth-like skin as the Bible progresses, fading to a blurry gender-neutral backdrop. To the contrary, the New Testament shows that complementarity is realized most gloriously in the union of the Savior, Jesus Christ, and His bride, the church. Every marriage is a little picture of this theologically wondrous truth. Every church is a living part of the bride of Christ, and awaits the consummation of this union in the age to come.

Conclusion
The teaching of the early chapters of Genesis means that every Christian—whether single or married—has the opportunity to savor life as a man or woman. Most of us

are called to marriage, and so the church must support and teach on marriage. Irrespective of our marital status, we must recognize that our manhood or womanhood is an integral part of our Christian identity. When saved by grace, we do not lose our manhood or womanhood, as poor readings of Galatians 3:27-28 sometimes suggest. Rather, we see our God-given sex as a crucial part of our identity, and resolve to give God maximal glory as a man or woman.

There is tremendous joy in this realization. God has made us either a man or a woman. God loves the shape, form, and function of manhood, and the shape, form, and function of womanhood. We do not acquire value when the opposite sex takes interest in us. We possess impossible amounts of dignity and worth as the people God formed for His own pleasure. It is appropriate and even essential that we live life attuned to the uniqueness of our God-made sex. We do not have to become famous or desired or valued to enjoy our existence. We may score epic goals or we may not; we may act on grand stages or we may not.

Whatever our vocation, we do not need anything from the world to secure a joyful, meaningful existence. We simply need to own God's design, give Him thanks for it, and live according to the script His Word gives us as Christian men and Christian women. The obedient life is the doxological life. The doxological life is the good life.

As men and women, the identity we crave is the one we already have: to be the creation of God, made according to His wise design, loved by a heavenly Father who gave His Son to make us His own.

CHAPTER TWO

What Is Biblical Manhood?

People often ask me what I miss most about playing professional football. They are surprised when I don't say, 'playing.' I had a long career but there are two things that I do miss. One is being super fit! The other is being with the guys in that dressing room. There is something special about men gathered together to play for a greater cause, where the cost is high and the reward is great. Therefore, in my ministry as a pastor at Calvary Grace Church in Calgary I have a burning desire to build men for the body of Christ. Manhood has been eclipsed in many places in our day, such that the truly biblical man is a rare species. This is tragic. When you lose men you lose the home, the church, and the culture. In this chapter, I want to define manhood through looking at a question and a challenge. First, we turn to the question that necessitates the challenge.

Adam, Where Are You? Abdication and The Man Crisis
We begin with words that are some of the most chilling in all Scripture.

> …Now the serpent was more crafty than any other beast of the field that the Lord God had made. He said to the woman, 'Did God actually say, "You shall not eat of any tree in the garden"?'… So when the woman saw that the tree was good for food, and that it was a delight to the eyes, and that the tree was to be desired to make one wise, she took of its fruit and ate, and *she also gave some to her husband who was with her, and he ate* (Gen. 3:1, 6).

We learn here of the abdication of Adam. Adam was made to be a leader. He was made first (Gen. 2:7). He was also given the moral mandate to work and keep the Garden and to eat from any tree except one (Gen. 2:15-17). As covered in Chapter One, Adam was given responsibility to name the animals and also the woman. The woman was made to be a helper for him to lead as they fitted together in God's design in line with God's desire to multiply His imagers across the earth. This is how the glory of God was to spread: through men and women, not just generically but particularly through their masculinity and femininity, physically and functionally. The roles were and are vital. The equality and difference are essential to maintain because it is in this synchronicity that God displays His glory in man.

But at the crucial point Adam flinched and went missing in action. He abdicated his responsibility to lead his wife when the serpent usurped the created order by approaching her first and not Adam. The roles reversed. She bit, he was passive, they both fell, creation was fractured, and relational crisis ensued. Firstly for Adam and Eve their relationship with God was broken; secondly their relationship with each other was broken.

And God came after Adam first. He said, Adam, 'Where are *you*?' (Gen. 3:9). He says to Adam, 'Cursed is the ground because of *you*' (Gen. 3:17). It didn't matter that Eve sinned first. It didn't matter that she was the main player of the two in the temptation scene in Eden. Adam was held primarily responsible. Adam was the head of the home and he abdicated his responsibility to protect his wife from the attack of the enemy, to provide a corrective word for her when she was getting God's Word wrong and to direct her back to truth and away from sin. He wimped out and remained passive. She led him, the serpent led her and both rebelled against God. Nevertheless, God calls Adam to account first.

Adam's response to God was a further illustration of abdication. 'You gave me that woman. It's her fault' is essentially his response (Gen. 3:12). He blamed her and more than that he blamed God. The abdication of masculine leadership is at the fall of mankind. First Adam failed to protect his wife. Then he failed to own his sin and repent. Instead, he acted like a guilty child, shifting the blame from himself to his wife. We see the pattern of domestic misery so familiar to the world already well established in the early chapters of Scripture. Sin begets sin, which begets bitterness, which leaves homes broken on the inside no matter what they look like on the outside.

From Genesis 3 onward, God raises up men to lead His people in different epochs of redemptive history. We see success when men lead well and failure where men passively avoid their responsibilities. At a particularly low point in Israel's history, God says through the prophet Ezekiel,

> And I sought for a man among them who should build up the wall and stand in the breach before me for the land, that I should not destroy it, but I found none. Therefore I have poured out my indignation upon them. I have consumed them with the fire of my wrath. I have returned their way upon their heads, declares the Lord God (Ezek. 22:30-31).

God is speaking here about His search for a man to take initiative, to intercede and to stand between the people and God's judgment that is coming. When a city was under siege, the men of the city were needed to breach any gaps in the wall in order to protect the people within. Now as then, God wants men who stand in the breach. He wants men who refuse to go quietly in the night, and will not allow women and children to suffer. He wants men like Abraham, Moses, Ezekiel and the Apostle Paul to stand in the gap, pray, and assume responsibility to lead themselves, their wives, children and churches away from the wrath of God and towards the grace of God in Christ.

Whether a man is unmarried or married, this biblical vision for manhood stands.

Jesus, the perfect man, was single, as was Paul. Marriage is a profound thing that pictures Christ and the Church, but marriage will not exist in heaven. Speaking of the resurrection, Jesus says, 'When the dead rise they will neither marry nor be given in marriage. They will be like the angels in heaven' (Mark 12:25). The final destiny is the marriage of Christ to His bride, the church (Rev. 19:1-11).

Mature manhood does not depend on being married. You don't become a man by getting married, and you certainly don't become a man by having sex, as traditional masculine cultures have often argued. Unregenerate manhood preys on women, weakening them and using them. Biblical manhood protects women, loving them through gracious leadership. Instead of taking from women as unsaved men do, godly men provide for women in appropriate ways, with the apex of this duty coming in marital provision (1 Tim. 5:8).[1]

The role of male and female, created equal in the image of God, but different in role by their design, is one of the crucial issues of our day. Where Satan has blurred the distinctions and subverted the roles we have a society which cannot answer the crucial question: what is a man? We find ourselves with a man crisis today. Darrin Patrick illustrates this in his book, *Church Planter*. He writes:

> We live in a world full of males who have prolonged their adolescence. They are neither boys nor men. They live, suspended as it were, between childhood and adulthood, between growing up and being grown-ups. Let's call this kind of male Ban, a hybrid of both boy and man.[2]

I resonate with Patrick's words. I coached high school football (soccer) for six years in Canada and I worked with a great number of young men from the age of 15-18. When they first came into the team, most of them lacked discipline, respect

---

1. For a fuller treatment of singleness see John Piper's foreword, 'For Single Men and Women (and the Rest of Us),' in *Recovering Biblical Manhood and Womanhood*, eds John Piper and Wayne Grudem (Wheaton: Crossway, 1991), xvii-xxviii.

2. Darrin Patrick, *Church Planter: The Man, The Message, The Mission* (Wheaton: Crossway, 2010), 9.

for authority and any sense of obligation to represent their families and schools. I soon discovered that 90 per cent of them had absent fathers: men who had either abandoned the home or, if they were at home, they were not involved in their sons' lives in any meaningful way. The result was boys: 'Bans,' as Patrick puts it. That's a tragedy for the young men themselves, but it's also a tragedy for young women, their families, and the future of society.

When my assistant coaches and I provided some discipline, a vision of what they could be and some care for them along the way, it was thrilling to see this school team win trophies year after year. These boys became men in the sporting arena. They could take setbacks and bounce back; they grew in self-control and could maintain their heads when others around were losing theirs; they could play for each other and the school, not just themselves. Sometimes I get an email from one of them telling me how much they appreciated those days and how it had benefitted them beyond high school. Manhood, they came to understand, meant the formation of character, not preying on girls or making money.

The Day of Judgment is coming and whilst each person is responsible for their own response to Christ, Christian men have a special responsibility to lead their wives, children and churches. Men are called to be leaders by very virtue of the fact that they are created male. This is not a competency issue. It is an issue of God's design. Yet this fact is lost on a growing number today in the broader realm. The further a society moves away from Scripture, the more it moves away from the things that the Scriptures define. Manhood is one key example of this.

Many boys have little sense of what it means to be a man, though they do know that a feminist culture rewards them for dampening their masculinity. Whether consciously or unconsciously, they adopt the traits of girls. Conversely, women today find themselves rewarded when they act in traditionally masculine ways. We think of the 'Dad Mom' phenomenon. Women go to work, men raise the kids. While fathers should love their families and be devoted to them, this new pattern is an inversion of the biblical design. A secular, gender-neutralizing culture only rewards men for this change. In this kind of context, we learn something sobering: there has never been an age when masculinity and femininity have been so confused.

We hear it in the homes, we hear it in the churches, and we hear it in the culture: an echo from Eden, 'Adam, where are you?' Where are the men? Thankfully, though we are in perilous times, manhood is not dead. There is hope for modern men, confused and listless as some are. Through the grace of Christ, men can change. But they need to be called to manhood and they need to be taught what manhood is.

Thus we turn from the question of Eden to the challenge of Corinth: 'Act like men.'

The Corinthian Challenge: Act Like Men

> Be watchful, stand firm in the faith, act like men,
> be strong. Let all that you do be done in love
> (1 Cor. 16:13-14).

Paul knows that the Christian life is war. He talks of fighting the good fight of faith (1 Tim. 6:12; 2 Tim. 4:7) and fighting against spiritual forces of evil in the heavenly realms (Eph. 6:12). The Christian life is spiritual warfare and he stresses a wartime mind-set in his last words to galvanize the church to action. His words in 1 Corinthians 16:13-14 apply to all believers, to be sure, but they have special significance for men, who are called to lead God's people, and thus are called to lead in exhibiting the five traits we explore below. In what follows, we seek to help men understand what they are to be in leading the flock of God.

First, Paul says to 'be watchful.'
Several years ago I was asked to speak to some young men at a college. The Resident Assistant told me what had given him the idea. He said, 'I was walking across campus one morning and I looked back at the dorms. It was 9:30 a.m. and the girls' blinds were all open, but the boys' blinds were all closed. The seriousness of the situation struck me then and there. And a cry arose within me, "Awake, O men of God".' In other words, biblical men are watchful, they are alert, they are sober, and they are awake.

There are strong biblical connections to this theme of 'watchfulness' as Paul terms it. The watchman in the Old Testament was like a lookout or spy. He would be in a high place with a broad view and his job was to stay awake and announce danger or threats to the people. This was a high-stakes affair. If he slept, he and the people could die.

Before we can care for others, we must recognize our need to take action in our own spiritual lives. Biblical men must be watchful of themselves. Life is war and we have an enemy. Peter says, 'Be sober-minded; be watchful. Your adversary the devil prowls around like a roaring lion, seeking someone to devour. Resist him firm in your faith...' (1 Pet. 5:8). Furthermore, Satan knows a man's weaknesses and sin is crouching at the door. A man may be redeemed but there is still a process of sanctification going on and he cannot afford to drift. A sleepy, peacetime mentality is what Satan wants. In the game of football—or soccer—there is a saying that goes, 'When you score a goal, you are at your most vulnerable for a goal against you for the next ten minutes.' Why? Because that's when you let your guard down and you're not on your toes.

Men must stay watchful over sin. They must get a 'clear view of the evil of sin'.[3] They should not live in a state of blind terror but should possess a healthy, godly fear of evil influences from the world and from within. Such influences are everywhere and they are seductive. A watchful man does not think himself impenetrable and immune to these things. Satan wants men and women to fall, but he particularly wants young men to struggle because as go the men, so go homes, churches, and even societies. The Apostle Paul says to the young Timothy, 'So flee youthful passions and pursue righteousness, faith, love, and peace, along with those who call on the Lord from a pure heart' (2 Tim. 2:22). This isn't an aimless panic but purposeful pursuing. Men, put distance between yourself and sin and head towards what is Christ-like.

A man without watchfulness is like a man without self-control; he is 'a city broken into and left without walls' (Prov. 25:28). He is vulnerable to attack and he leaves those in his care in peril. A man must be watchful over his spiritual state. He must pay attention to his character. If he falls, his wife and the family will fall with him. If an elder falls, there is widespread fallout in the church.

---

3. J. C. Ryle, *Thoughts For Young Men* (Merrick, New York: Calvary Press, 1996), 41. Bishop Ryle speaks of the need for young men to get a clear view of the evil of sin by 'thinking' what the Bible says about sin, what change it has made in a man, what atonement cost, what are the effects of sin upon the earth, and what is the misery and sorrow it has caused.

Biblical men must also be watchful over single women, wives, and children.[4]

Biblical manhood means leadership and leadership means watchful protection and provision for women. This kind of leadership is life-preserving. Just as Adam was given the leadership task in creation, a husband is to sacrificially protect his wife (Eph. 5:25), fathers must watch over their children (Eph. 6:4), and qualified men should lead the church (1 Tim. 2:12, 1 Tim. 3, Titus 1). And here in 1 Corinthians is a general call for all men to be watchful.

Men were made to work and *physically provide*. A lazy man who is not alert does not deserve to eat (2 Thess. 3:10), and those in his care will suffer. And he who stays home and watches the children while his wife goes out to work is not fulfilling his manly mandate. It doesn't matter if she has more earning power; it's about God's design for manhood. There may be a season where a wife must step in to help, or a man may have disabilities that preclude him from certain labour. For men in general, however, the inclination to provide should be there. The biblical man's job is physical provision.

The watchful man should have a sense of *physical protection* towards women. In an age where many countries put women on the frontline in war, we have lost this perspective. Yet one must ask, would a noble husband send his wife downstairs to confront the intruder who has just broken in? The answer is clear. Men must physically protect women, for no other reason than because they are men. Men must put their lives on the line, whenever necessary, to care for women and children.

---

4. To grow as a husband in this and other areas, see Stuart Scott, *Exemplary Husband: A Biblical Perspective* (Bemidji, MN: Focus Publishing, 2002).

A biblical man must also *protect and provide spiritually* for his wife. He must lead her in devotions, seeking to be like Jesus, who washed His bride with the Word of God (Eph. 5:26). This requires a man to regularly sit down with his wife and bring her a nugget from God's Word and apply it to her, as he lives with her in an understanding way (1 Pet. 3:7). (I will expand on this in Chapter 4). A man must know what God demands of him as the head of his wife and he needs to know his wife's spiritual needs. He should be watchful to protect her spiritual progress, encouraging and even correcting if necessary. This spiritual provision should extend to the family as he leads in family devotions.

Second, Paul says to 'stand firm in the faith.'

To grasp this truth, we must fix this in our minds: biblical men are men of the Word. If a man is going to stand firm in a war against the world, the flesh and the devil, he needs a weapon in his armoury. The Word is the Sword of the Spirit and men at war need to know it and memorize it so when the devil attacks or when sinful impulses arise they can fight back. Men need to take up the Bible and meditate upon it (Ps. 1). J. C. Ryle exhorts us to this Word-work: 'Settle it down in your mind as an established rule, that, whether you feel it at the moment or not, you are inhaling spiritual health by reading the Bible, and insensibly becoming more strong.'[5]

Men must put up protections and avoid temptation, but sin is ultimately defeated by believing the promises of God in His Word over the promise of pleasure in the sin. In Matthew 4, when Jesus is in the wilderness and Satan tempts Him, each

---

5. J. C. Ryle, *Practical Christianity* (Cambridge: James Clark & Co., Ltd., 1970), 98.

time Jesus answers him, 'It is written...' He fights Satan by faith in the Word of God.

The man who tries by willpower alone to avoid giving in to lust, whether that is pornography or adultery or the lure of a mental sexual fantasy world, will eventually capitulate. But the moment of temptation when Satan is whispering about the pleasure awaiting and sinful impulses are rising up is when the biblical man unsheathes the sword of God's Word. He believes the promise of Jesus to be with him to the end of the age (Matt. 28:20), even trusting that He is with him in that moment and the man turns away from sin and Satan and towards Christ in faith. Sin is severed at its root and Satan flees from the man of faith.

Biblical men are also men of prayer. The gospel writer, Mark, says of Christ: 'And rising very early in the morning, while it was still dark, he departed and went out to a desolate place, and there he prayed' (Mark 1:35). When Jesus was at His busiest, He went to be alone with God. From where did Jesus get His power for ministry? From communion with His Father in prayer. Though He was fully God, He lived as a man in the power of the Spirit.

The mark of the man of God is the mark of God upon the man. Manhood is in great part about being a man of prayer. Prayer displays dependency upon God. Far from being self-sufficient, men of God are desperate and weak. When I was small I jumped into the swimming pool on vacation without my arm-bands (water wings). I started to go under, so my father sprinted from his chair and dived into the water and scooped me up as I was going down. I was offered ice cream and chocolate to comfort me afterwards, but I would have none of it. I just clung to my dad. He was my source of life and I would not let him go. That's the kind of desperation God seeks from us in prayer. Like

Jacob we must desperately wrestle with God in prayer and say, 'I will not let you go until you bless me' (Gen. 32:26).

A biblical man spends time with God and he is a biblical man to the extent that he does this. This is a strong statement, but a needed one. He is on his knees, seeking God's will and glory, praying for holiness, praying for his wife and children, praying for his ministry, praying for his church and nation. He sees this as his holy responsibility. He enjoys God's common grace gifts, but he structures his life so that he can pray and study Scripture.[6] Those observing his life will say, 'He is a man captured by God. He is not obsessed with culture or sports or entertainment. He is driven, fundamentally, to know God.'[7]

A biblical man is a divine, not a dude. He is a man of weight and substance, like the great Scottish Reformer John Knox of whom Mary, Queen of Scots, reputedly said, 'I fear the prayers of John Knox more than all the assembled armies of Europe.'[8] Biblical men are Knox-like men. They know what they believe and know their God. They stand firm because they are men of the Word and prayer. They are powerful not because of their weight-lifting exploits but because they have drawn near to God, and He has drawn near to them (James 4:8).[9]

---

6. This kind of man practices what is now called 'family ministry.' For a helpful introduction, see Randy Stinson and Timothy Paul Jones, *Trained in the Fear of God: Family Ministry in Theological, Historical, and Practical Perspective* (Grand Rapids, MI: Kregel Academic & Professional, 2011).

7. A great book for men to read and study with their families is Bruce Ware, *Big Truths for Young Hearts: Teaching and Learning the Greatness of God* (Wheaton, IL: Crossway, 2009).

8. See Bruce Atkinson, *Land of Hope and Glory: British Revival Through the Ages* (London: Dovewell, 2003), 57.

9. I recommend David McIntyre, *The Hidden Life of Prayer* (Ross-shire, Scotland: Christian Focus, 1989)—an immense help in developing my personal communion with God.

Third, Paul says to 'act like men.'

Here is the central command: "act like men," not like boys and not like women. Even as he calls all believers to maturity, Paul recognises that there is a specific way that a man should act, with manly bravery. This is not a call to be macho but to be mature. Men can be jocks, artists, businessmen, musicians, it matters not. What matters is this: are you serious about God? Again, we need divines not dudes: men like the Puritans who knew God and had a sense of the weight of His glory upon them.

There's time for fun, but the stakes are too high in this life to be silly. Some men are always joking with the boys and getting drawn into the crudities of 'dressing room' banter. They talk about women as objects of lust. They never seem to grow up.

The church and the world need men of substance, sober-minded not sombre. Such men think clearly about their identity as men not women, and then ponder how they can act as men in relation to women. Whilst recognising the equality of the sexes, they seek to delineate the difference. They act like men by treating women differently than men. They are not effeminate. They act like men with a masculine moral courage and bravery, which takes responsibility and doesn't wallow in self-pity. Mature manhood inclines toward action and isn't paralysed by passivity.

Acting like a man also means decision-making. We'll talk about this later in the book in relation to marriage, but there is a great need for young men to learn to make decisions. This is all part of the masculine mandate to exercise lordship. Whilst the command to 'subdue' and 'have dominion' was given to both the man and the woman (Gen. 1:27), there is a primacy of lordship given to the man. We see this as Adam names the animals (Gen. 2:19-20). But note that God brought the animals to him 'to see what he would call them' (Gen. 2:19). God wanted Adam to exercise his authority and decide on the names. Procrastination and indecision ruin a man, but God-fearing decisiveness makes him.[10]

Boys blame-shift like Adam in the garden. Men take responsibility for their sin and desperately cling to their identity in Christ. This is where there is a great need for role models, because manhood is taught—but manhood is also caught. When I began as a young professional footballer in 1984, we apprentices were given all the hard jobs that no-one wanted to do. Clean the dressing rooms, pick up all the sweaty, bloody kit, and polish the boots of the pros and so on. And you were expected to do these chores without complaint because if you moaned or showed disrespect to the senior professionals, they would close the dressing room door and sort you out by verbal, or sometimes physical discipline. You learned to take criticism and you proved your manhood.

But I saw change over the years and by the end of my career some young apprentices who had not been fathered, mentored or taught manhood would come in with a sense of entitlement. They wore nice clothes and drove nice cars before they had ever achieved anything. If they were asked to clean the boots it was half-hearted at best. And if they were criticised they were very defensive.

Biblical men are not entitled boys with precious egos; they can give and take criticism well. They submit to leadership and they learn from other mature men. Here's where a culture of mentoring needs to be developed throughout a

---

10. Mark Chanski has two chapters that deal insightfully with the issue of wisdom in decision-making. See Chanski, *Manly Dominion: In a Passive-Purple-Four-Ball World* (Merrick, New York: Calvary Press, 2014), 107-130.

church. Manhood must be taught and spiritual friendships among men provide the context for the older mentoring the younger. [11]

Fourth, Paul says to 'be strong.'
Biblical men go towards the battle, do hard things, and work hard. Men don't have time to self-pity, whilst women pick up the slack. Satan's tactics are subtle and he will use what he can to make a man procrastinate. Theodore Roosevelt's father famously urged his son to 'Get action!' He encouraged him to be proactive not reactive. A man who makes lists and does things in order of importance is a man who studies and has dominion over his life. This means taking control of his appetites in the areas of food, drink, and sex.

But the strength a biblical man needs is gospel-driven strength. Paul says, 'By the grace of God I am what I am and his grace towards me was not in vain. Nevertheless I worked harder than any of them. Yet it was not I but the grace of God in me' (1 Cor. 15:10). Paul is saying that he has been so changed by Christ, and that Christ strengthens him so much that he is able to work harder than anyone else for the strength of Christ in him allows him to do so. This fuels a sense of responsibility to work and take risks because the motivation and strength is Christ, not selfish gain.

The biblical man is the man his wife can lean on. He is a man of his word and a man of integrity. Others in the family, church and neighborhood can rely on him for strength and support. Like a massive tree, he won't easily snap and crack.

---

11. Albert Mohler has done tremendous work on helping boys to mature. See R. Albert Mohler, Jr., *From Boy to Man: The Marks of Manhood* (Louisville: SBTS Publications, 2005), accessible at http://www.sbts.edu/wp-content/uploads/sites/5/2010/09/boy-to-man.pdf.

You can trust him. He is the sort of person who forms a plan for his family, shows up early to begin executing the plan, and keeps morale high as he leads others to the goal. He's not passive, asking his wife to do the heavy-lifting. He gladly solicits her wisdom, but he takes it upon himself to plan, execute, and see things through. This is the kind of guy who looks you in the eye, says what he means, and gets done what he says he will get done.

This isn't a case of 'come on guys, pull your socks up and be macho.' This is a case of 'realize the amazing resource you have in Christ as a new creation and act.' The biblical man derives his power from the work of Christ. Paul assumes this when he exhorts the Corinthians, but beneath his exhortation is a super-heated engine of grace. Christ crucified and resurrected, united to us by the Spirit, takes men of weakness and makes them men of action. Strength is essential for men at war and the strength they need is supernatural. It will enable movement towards and through hard things.

Fifth, Paul says to 'Let all you do be done in love.'
You might have heard that manhood reduces to feats of testosterone. But in Paul's Spirit-inspired mind, the flavour of true manhood is this: love. Paul says in 1 Corinthians 13:3, 'If I give all I possess to the poor and give over my body to hardship that I may boast, but do not have love, I gain nothing.' He gives the apostolic goal in 1 Timothy, 'The aim of our charge is love' (1 Tim. 1:5).

Love for God and love for neighbor are the two greatest commands (Matt. 22:34-39). A biblical man loves God above all else and is passionate for His purposes. He is a man who is radically transformed by the love of God in the gospel; a God who, in love, sends His Son to willingly bear sin on the cross and as a substitute to exhaust the wrath of God due to sinners; a God who in love counts sinful men righteous because of the righteous life of His Son; a God who, in love, rescues men destined for Hell and makes them sons and heirs; a God who, in love, offers this freely to any who will repent and trust in Him.

Biblical men know this kind of love and gratefully display this love in service to women. It's this kind of love that drives men not out of guilt or duty, but out of desire for God's glory. It's this kind of love that will make a man's leadership firm but gracious, strong but gentle, tender-hearted but firm. God wants men who are authoritative, but not authoritarian. Paul's fifth exhortation is a challenge to surrender to Christ and show Christ-like love. Without this kind of love, obedience to the previous commands will be harsh. Men must be like Christ in the way they exercise their authority; lionhearted and lamblike with meekness and majesty. This is the virtue that will characterize all biblical masculinity.

And this is the kind of leadership that Paul calls husbands to in Ephesians 5. He tells husbands they are the heads because they are men (Eph. 5:23). It's just what kind of head they are. That's the question. So that's why he says, 'Husbands love your wives as Christ loved the church and gave himself up for her' (Eph. 5:25). This is a challenge for a man to die to self for the good of his wife. Extending the principle, a biblical man dies for others, especially women. He is a giver. He is generous. He knows his God and where he is going and what his manly purpose is and with Paul he says, 'To live is Christ and to die is gain....I will continue with all of you for your progress and joy in the faith' (Phil. 1:21, 25). He will suffer for the good of others.

The man of God also loves the spread of the gospel. In his message on 'Men and Missions: The Missing Link' at the

2014 CBMW National Conference in Louisville, Danny Akin stated that there are approximately 6,500 unreached people groups today. That's 3.6-4.7 billion who will live, die and go to hell without hearing the name of Jesus. He went on to produce alarming statistics that showed that women significantly outnumber men on the mission field. Debt, pornography, parental pressure (men capitulate to pressure of mother or father), materialism, recognition and praise, and faulty theology that breed intellectual arrogance rather than a missionary heart, are all reasons that men retreat according to Akin.[12]

We give thanks for brave Christian women who devote their lives to the spread of the gospel. We're cheering them on! But if only they go and men stay home, we must know that the weakness of men ends up presenting a feminised and under-resourced Christianity to the world. Men were made to lead in God's mission. With Eve as his helper, that was Adam's job; to work, keep and extend the borders of Eden filling the world with imagers of God. And in the New Testament Jesus gives the Great Commission to the disciples; men who would assume the challenge of His mission to take God's glory to the nations through the spread of the gospel. Love for God's glory must extend to love for God's people and love for God's fame amongst all the nations.

Men must rediscover this kind of love, a love that moves you forward, that compels you to be watchful, to stand firm in the faith, to act like men and to be strong. This kind of love views singleness or marriage, having children or careers, for the glory of God amongst the nations. Only this kind of

---

12. Dr Akin's talk can be found at http://cbmw.org/uncategorized/cbmw-national-conference-media. See his stirring book on this subject: Akin, *Five Who Changed the World* (Wake Forest: Southeastern Seminary, 2008).

love will motivate a man to give his life away, so that he can say with the martyred missionary Jim Elliot, 'He is no fool who gives what he cannot keep to gain that which he cannot lose.'[13]

We should hear God's call afresh: *Adam, where are you?* We should remember also that the second Adam, Jesus Christ, has answered for you and me. He came forth to suffer our punishment and to redeem our masculinity and empower us to be the men of God that we must be. God made a promise in Genesis 3:15 to send one who would crush the head of the serpent. And in the fullness of time He sent His own Son who won victory at Calvary over Satan, sin and death and who rose and ascended victorious and who will come again as Judge and King.

The hard truth is this: all men have failed like Adam. I have failed. You have failed. This is lamentable, but it is also part of life in a fallen world populated, without exception, by sinners. The good news for us men, men of clay, is this: because of Christ's victory, all Christians can obey the Corinthian Challenge, and men of God can lead in exemplifying the kind of character Paul calls for in 1 Cor. 16. His charge to 'act like men' shows us that he has in mind that men will play their God-given part in cultivating cruciform courage so that the church will be led well.

We ourselves know our weaknesses all too well. As we reencounter Paul's words, we know that we will not be perfect. It is our utmost desire, however, to be faithful. We recognize that such growth in godliness is not an option, but a commission. If God's church is to be strong, we must grow

---

13. Jim Elliot, *The Journals of Jim Elliot*, ed. Elisabeth Elliot (Grand Rapids: Revell, 2002), 174.

strong in Christ, and lead well in the household of God. Let us seize this truth once more and display something greater to the world than passivity, selfishness, and weakness.

Brothers, let us act like men.

CHAPTER THREE

What is Biblical Womanhood?

I was present when both my children were born. They were joyful and thrilling occasions. My wife was 48 hours in grueling labor with our son, Jake, and mercifully not as long with our daughter, Ava. It was an amazing thing to see the strength and courage of my wife and the miracle of a new life, which she had received, nurtured, and grown inside her body for nine months.

Throughout each pregnancy I watched as her belly grew and began to move from the inside out with an alien-like leg or arm looking like it was trying to break out. I used to ask her, 'Doesn't that feel weird?' and she would answer, 'It feels like the most natural thing in the world.' All the time I was thinking, 'I'm glad I don't have to do this!' However, the obvious thing is, I was not made to do this. Never were our differences more vividly displayed than when Amanda gave birth to our children. She was made to give life.

Of course, a woman is firstly made to worship and glorify God. But she does this by fulfilling God's specific purpose for her as a woman. God owns her, so God defines her and instructs her in her task. My wife was created as my equal, but made with a very different body than mine. The physical differences underpin functional differences based on a difference in sex. She was made female to receive, nurture and grow life, and I was not. She was made to be a life giver like Eve, the first woman, who was called 'the mother of all the living' (Gen. 3:20). And this life-giving role extends beyond physically giving birth. Design shows us a great deal about our God-given calling.

In this chapter, we consider the essence of life-giving biblical womanhood. As we go, we see how counter-cultural and God-honoring womanhood truly can be. Our study unfolds in three sections:

1) The Role: A Helper, Not A Hindrance
2) The Attitude: Reverent Womanhood
3) The Response: Submission Under Sovereignty.

The Role: A Helper, Not A Hindrance

The best football teams I played in were the ones in which each player was placed in his best position within the team. Each person had a specific role. I remember Kevin Keegan, the Newcastle Utd manager (head coach), sitting me down in his office one day and showing me our team on a tactics board. 'Just look at my team,' he said. 'When the goalie gets it he throws it to the fullback. The center-backs drop deep, one midfielder shows for the ball, one winger stays wide, and one striker comes deep whilst the other one runs in behind the opposition defense. Look how we fit together and move up the field.'

Keegan was painting a picture of this machine he was building on the football pitch. The point was, everyone knew their position and fulfilled their role in that machine. This well-oiled machine won promotion to the Premier League that season. There was order and harmony. Everyone knew his purpose. And it is that way with God's picture in creation for a woman.

What specifically was the woman created for? She was a 'helper fit for him' (Gen. 2:18, 20). This was the unique role given by God to Eve. Adam was not created as a helper for Eve (Gen. 2:18-22 cf. 1 Cor. 11:9-11). As noted in Chapter One, God created male and female equally in His image. He made Adam first but it was not good for him to be alone (Gen. 2:18). He needed someone to help him to complete the commission to be fruitful and multiply and rule over creation (Gen. 1: 28). The woman was to help him do this by producing children with him and filling the earth with the presence of God's image bearers. She was the man's second in command.

So Eve functions as Adam's helper by virtue of creation. The Bible refers to God as our Helper but God is not created.[1] However, Eve is a 'helper *fit for him.*' That is to say, she corresponds to Adam as one made in God's image like him. And she is created with the specific purpose of being his helper. The Hebrew text of Genesis 2:18 can be

---

1. See Ray Ortlund's essay, 'Male-Female Equality and Male Headship,' *Recovering Biblical Manhood and Womanhood* (Wheaton: Crossway, 1991), 95-112. Ortlund includes a treatment of the meaning of 'helper' on page 104.

translated literally, 'I will make *for him* a helper fit for him.' The Apostle Paul follows this flow of thought when he writes in 1 Corinthians 11:9, 'Neither was man created *for* woman, but woman *for* man.' Eve's role, and the purpose was to be a helper to her husband.[2]

In addition, God emphasizes that the woman is not to help the man as one who is inferior to him. Rather, she is to be a helper 'fit for him' and here the Hebrew word, *kenegdô*, means 'corresponding to him,' or 'equal and adequate to himself.' So Eve was created as a helper, but as a helper who was Adam's equal, who differed from him but complemented him.[3]

We are either male or female—not one singular sex or something in between, but binary sexes—male and female by creation. It is also clear from Genesis 1 that God values both men and women the same. There is no superior sex, and both are created in His image and given a common mandate (Gen. 1:27-28). But equality of personhood doesn't demand uniform sameness. Just like each player is equal but fulfills a different role within the football team, God designed our equality to be expressed differently in the way we relate to each other as men and women. The Bible explains that equality of value does not mean unlimited equality. God purposefully made distinctions between men and women that were not just biological. They are rooted in the very image of God stamped on the soul of a man and woman. God wants to say something more about Himself through the differences between the sexes. This flies in the face of our culture, which equates value and dignity with role and authority. It argues that the more

---

2. These ideas are expressed well by Wayne Grudem, *Evangelical Feminism and Biblical Truth* (Wheaton: Crossway, 2004), 119.

3. Ibid, 119.

authority you have, the more value you have. This is not true, though. The president has more authority than the people but is of no more value than they. The elders and the congregation are of the same value but one submits to the other's authority (Heb. 13:17). So it is with a husband and wife and parents and children. Children are not inferior to their parents as human beings. They are fully human and loaded with dignity and worth. But they do not possess the authority of their parents, and they do not possess the role of their parents.

Where the principle of equating value with authority gains ground, disorder will ensue. Rebellion against authority is rife in our egalitarian day. Some congregations now consider elders to be 'hired hands', not divinely called, biblically qualified men who are to shepherd and lead with authority (1 Pet. 5:1-4). Some parents functionally submit to their child's wishes. Some teachers lack power to discipline their students. Some wives chafe against their husband's God-given role as head of the home. Turn on the television, and chances are good you'll see a reality-TV star or celebrity finding a way to rebel against something, and seeking applause for their behavior. Rebellion against authority is lauded in our age.

Secular culture may despise authority and undermine it at every turn. But this will not do for Christians who have submitted to God, and this will not do for women of God who love divine design. Eve is second in the created order. She is called to follow Adam. She is made for him, specifically as his helper. To unlock this discovery is to unleash part of the wonder of femininity. Women and men are not the same. Women are relieved from the burden of pretending they are men, and trying to be men, as feminism would instruct them. Women who love the Lord will find tremendous freedom, hope and purpose in embracing the wise plan of God for women.[4] This is no inferior life that the Creator offers Eve's sisters. This is the good life, the Godward life, the life that brings happiness through obedience.

The way God created the woman speaks to His tender love for her. Genesis 2:21-22 causes us to marvel at His work: 'So the LORD God caused a deep sleep to fall upon the man, and while he slept, took one of his ribs and closed up its place with flesh. And the rib that the LORD God had taken from the man he made into a woman and brought her to the man.' Eve's formation is not exactly parallel to Adam's. Adam was made from dust. Eve was made from his rib and is derivative from him. She was taken out of man.

Modern feminism wants women to see themselves as independent from men and wants men to see themselves as independent from women.[5] It not only wants to flatten the distinctions between the sexes, though. It wants to turn them away from each other. But it is so beautifully clear that God wants us to see that we are profoundly connected to each other. There is mutual interdependence here in a much richer and deeper way than in any secular gender theory.

We see this relationship in 1 Corinthians 11:11-12. There, Paul explicitly disavows the idea that the sexes are cut off from one another: 'Nevertheless, in the Lord woman is not independent of man nor man of woman; for as woman was made from man, so man is now born of woman.' This means that the woman depends on the man for life, and a

---

4. See Mary A. Kassian, *Girls Gone Wise in a World Gone Wild* (Chicago, IL: Moody Publishers, 2010).

5. See Mary A. Kassian, *The Feminist Mistake: The Radical Impact of Feminism on Church and Culture* (Wheaton, IL: Crossway, 2005); Margaret Elizabeth Köstenberger, *Jesus and the Feminists: Who Do They Say That He Is?* (Wheaton, IL: Crossway, 2008).

man can only be born through a woman. Men have no place lording themselves over women as if they do not need women. Their very life depended in every way on a woman when in the womb. They were helpless, fed by a woman's nutrients, kept safe by a woman's unique frame. What a challenge to the overactive male ego this is. Men and women depend on one another in vital, God-made ways.

For their part, women are life-givers. Women give physical life to humanity, a task so great and so significant it cannot be quantified. God has highly esteemed women by making the survival of the human race hang on their care and nurture. There is immense fulfillment and meaning for women in this truth.

A fallen world ruled by a fallen angel seeks to turn women away from God's good design for women. We see why Satan would foment support for abortion. By targeting children in the womb, he guts a key part of the glory of womanhood. He ruins an incredible gift of God. Not only does he rob God of His glory, he robs many women of their identity in turning them against the child inside them. We must never think that it is God who devalues women. In giving them the chance to nurture and bear life, He has granted them a great privilege, one at which they should marvel.

In a nature-denying age, many women today are confused about their calling in life. They have been told that childraising is a lesser call than earning money in the marketplace, and so they should 'lean in' at work. Facebook COO Sheryl Sandberg, for example, has written approvingly of her very busy workday.[6] She seems to view it as her chief privilege that she gets to log back into email for several hours after a brief

---

6. See Sheryl Sandberg, *Lean In: Women, Work, and the Will to Lead* (New York: Knopf, 2013).

spell with her children. Here's one thing everyone can agree on: if answering email is the good life, it's probably worth 'leaning out!'

Many young women, influenced by the sexual revolution, struggle today. They have been told the good life is pursuing a career, having sex when one desires ('Netflix and chill,' it's called), and traveling wherever one wants to go. Some women are called to be single, and so a career may be in the offing. But many—most—women are called to marriage and motherhood. They will find happiness and deep satisfaction in this way of life. There is in the heart of a woman a nurturing instinct, one that the culture today sneers at. Women do well not to quieten this ability, but to use it, whether that means making a family as a married woman or caring for the children of church members and friends as a single woman. Women are not able to be womanly only when they are married with kids. They may richly glorify God by nurturing life in myriad contexts—church, as part of their vocation, friends, and more. It's not that there are too few contexts to use womanly gifts. It's that there are too many to count.

Womanhood is to be celebrated, not avoided. In Genesis 2:23-24, Adam celebrates the creation of woman. As God, who is literally the first father of the bride, brings her to the man, there is delight in Adam's words when he sees her (think of a groom seeing his bride come down the aisle!). He addresses God with words of joy. He doesn't see her as his competitor but as his complement. This scene climaxes in a one-flesh marriage of covenant love. 'And the man and his wife were both naked and were not ashamed' (Gen. 2:24). That they were naked and unashamed doesn't mean Adam had a great six-pack and Eve was a supermodel! It means there was perfect and pure covenant love. So nothing was between them. There was no rivalry, no chafing or challenging for position or power, but a complementary relationship, which mirrors the very relationship of authority and submission, love and harmony, in the Trinity.

Paul explains this parallel in 1 Cor. 11:3 'But I want you to understand that the head of every man is Christ, the head of a wife is her husband, and the head of Christ is God.' The Son does the Father's will: 'I do exactly as the Father commanded me,' Christ said in John 14:31. He submitted Himself to the Father's will (John 6:38). This posture of submission to fatherly authority did not begin the day Jesus came to earth. The Father *is* the authority of Christ, and always has been. The Son joyfully carries out the plan of His Father. The persons of the Godhead are not impersonal, with only titles to differentiate them. They are living *persons*, and their own love has structure and form. The Father as Father has authority; the Son as Son obeys His Father.[7]

Just as there is equality of value but difference in authority and role in the Trinity, so it is with husband and wife. Of course, no husband or wife is divine. But the point is clear: in the home, God creates order for the purpose of harmony. A wife is to be a helper, not a hindrance, to her husband. This means her primary task is to help him accomplish his plans for the family. But his plans must be God's plans and she is to help him discover what that is in particular for their marriage and family. As a helper she is his greatest counselor, and if he is a good leader he will solicit that counsel in forming his vision.

---

7. To understand the persons and roles of the Godhead better, see Bruce A. Ware, *Father, Son, and Holy Spirit: Relationships, Roles, and Relevance* (Wheaton, IL: Crossway, 2005); also Bruce A. Ware and John Starke, eds., *One God in Three Persons: Unity of Essence, Distinction of Persons, Implications for Life* (Wheaton, IL: Crossway, 2015).

A wife can help to draw leadership out of her husband by graciously engaging him. This does not mean jumping in where there is a void. It means prayerfully waiting for him to act and, if necessary, encouraging him to take the lead. A wife should look to her husband as her leader. The pattern in the home is one of masculine initiation, even as husbands will at times lead by having their wife suggest a course to try. He welcomes her input, even as she welcomes his guidance.

Some wives may not realize why they are so tired. It could be that they are doing too much leading and not enough helping and he is not doing enough leading and too much helping. It's often the same in the church. Men need to initiate and take the burden and women need to step back and help them. The balance needs to shift. As a woman obeys God's pattern she will feel freer and more feminine.

Women are just as gifted as men. There is, though, a functional difference that channels the use of each sex's gifts. Notice in Genesis that the man names her out of his own understanding of her as woman, from man. His name indicates to her that her own identity is related to him: she is from his own body. So we see how the sexes have relational identities. We individually bear the full image of God, but we do this always in relation to our identity as men or women. So it is in the Trinity: the Father is not the Son but He is called the Father because He is in relation to the Son and vice versa. In a similar way, the woman is not a man but is called a woman in relation to a man and vice versa.

What about unmarried women? Are they *fully* women of God? Some single women sadly feel inadequate, but this mindset does not stem from the Scripture. A woman doesn't become a biblical woman when she gets married, in the same way that a man doesn't need marriage to be masculine. Single womanhood is not a sin; it is a gift (1 Cor. 7). But Christ came as a single man to redeem single women and married women and bring them into one family (the church) and one marriage—bridegroom to bride. In this family, women are sisters in relation to brothers. Every godly woman, single or married, is defined by her God-given womanhood, not her marital status.

The fulfillment of being a helper comes first through marriage. It does not rely solely on being married or bearing children, however. After all, a Christian mother trains her daughter to be like Eve, and so the root identity of 'helper' comes, ideally, long before marriage. We cannot easily switch off this identity. Godly girls are being trained to assume this role well before they enter it formally in a marriage.

Christian women in the church need not try to imitate men, but can instead highlight the masculinity of men by being feminine. A single woman can be feminine with all men at all times appropriate to her relationship with them. In this way she is helping men to be masculine. She should be neither flirtatious nor forceful but feminine in the ways we are unpacking in this chapter. Also, all Christian women have the privilege of channeling their helping role in becoming spiritual mothers.[8] This is a major blessing, and one that we often underplay.

What does biblical womanhood mean in the modern workplace, though? What if you are a woman in a position of leadership over men? Care and discernment are needed here. A fallen world presents us with many tough questions, and we need wisdom and counsel from godly elders to answer these

---

8. Sharon James has a useful chapter on the fulfillment of the helper role and ministry in the church for married and single women, *God's Design For Women: Biblical Womanhood For Today* (Evangelical Press, 2002), 77-91.

questions. However precisely we answer, the point is this: Christian womanhood should have meaning in the workplace as well as the home and church. This means you express your femininity in all of life in all relationships. So young women should think carefully about what kind of job they might be working towards. Will it demand a masculine, directive aggression that goes against the grain of femininity? A woman's challenge is to avoid a thin, quasi-womanhood, which doesn't embrace the fullness of her feminine vocation and presents what Elisabeth Elliot calls a 'pseudo-personhood.'[9]

Surely, there are ambiguities on the matter of women in the workplace. I would suggest, though, that there are certain jobs which would at some point stretch biblical femininity to such an extent that they would be untenable for her (or reversely a man). An army sergeant for instance—barking orders and directing men or a female referee in a football match.

It's not that a woman cannot lead in any instance. In some cases, she must lead, making decisions and setting a vision (see Proverbs 31). But even when she leads, she does so in a feminine way (like Deborah in Judges 4). Her leadership, further, cannot help but look different from that of a secular, feminist culture which holds no stake in Christian femininity. The way a godly woman interacts with male colleagues will stand out in a non-Christian environment, for women of Christ value men and do not seek to demean them.

The key to these questions lies as much in training as it does in situational decision-making. Long before a single young woman faces complex vocational questions, she should hear regularly about the goodness of marriage, motherhood, and homemaking. It is a good thing for girls to be trained

---

9. Elisabeth Elliot, *Let Me Be A Woman* (Tyndale, 1976), 45.

intellectually for work, for no parent knows their daughter's future. She may need to provide for herself, and having training will help. But Christian parents need to think carefully with their daughters about college, taking on massive debt as many families do today, and whether their girls will be able—should God allow—to become a wife, mother, and homemaker.

The standard twenty-first-century Western practice of raising boys and girls in exactly the same way does not align with biblical principles. Again, these are matters that require discernment and much prayer. But our point stands: Christians must be careful to raise their girls in distinctly biblical ways that will give them freedom to receive the vocation God eventually gives them—and not tie them down for years in unfulfilling payment of excruciating debt in service to a career that no longer glitters.

Biblical womanhood, we see, takes work. The TV series *Downton Abbey* recently did a 'behind the scenes' documentary on what made the program so popular. One of the reasons given was its attention to the detail of the Edwardian day in which it is set. The program historian hosted the documentary. He explained that his role is to direct the actors in what they should wear and how they should conduct themselves. In the time in which the show was originally set there was order and role and etiquette between the sexes. He commented that although this was hard work for the actors, it was effortless for the Edwardians. It was effortless because they were trained in these things from a young age.

When a woman views herself as God's possession made for God's purpose, then womanhood is about godliness and serving in myriad ways is something to be embraced. But it takes work, spiritual sweat. Though a woman is born female, the culture has lost sight of what feminine behavior looks like.

Women need to work at and teach womanhood because we have lost our way in a sexually confused and perverse society that says no to God's design for women and thereby does women damage.

Christian women can be a counter-culture to the womanhood that secular culture promotes. Christian women have a far higher goal than that which our world sets for them: to glorify God *as a woman*. This involves being a helper—first in the context of marriage, and then as a principle to apply in her broader life. Godly womanhood takes training. And the training must start from the inside out. We think here of 1 Timothy 4:7, where Paul tells Timothy and his church to 'train yourself for godliness.' Such is the calling of a godly woman.

The Attitude: Reverent Womanhood

Inside a biblical woman is an attitude of respect for masculine, sacrificial leadership. To put it another way, reverence is the key posture of womanhood. In teaching this truth, Scripture contains many examples of disrespectful women. One of the most memorable is Job's wife, who told him to 'curse God and die' (Job 2:9) in the midst of his suffering. Instead of helping him and supporting her leader who was taking the full force of Satan's attacks, she hinders him. Job graciously rebukes her by telling her she is speaking like one of the 'foolish women' (Job 2:10). It is foolish and dangerous to be a disrespectful woman.

The Bible also contains many examples of respectful women: Bathsheba who bowed down to David (1 Kings 1:31) or Esther whose respectful tone won the king's ear (Esther 5:4). And Sarah who 'obeyed Abraham, calling him lord' (1 Pet. 3:6). And in Titus 2 we have a picture of mature womanhood: 'Older women likewise are to be reverent in behavior,' Paul says in Titus 2:3. In Titus 2, womanly ministry is about mature women, mothers and wives instructing less mature women in womanhood. Reverence is where it starts, because the inner attitude produces the right actions. This particular word for reverent (*hieroprepes*) occurs only here in the NT. It means 'like a priestess.' A biblical woman conducts herself like a priestess at all times with a conscious awareness of the all-seeing eye of God.

A reverent woman is not assertive, loud and obnoxious. She is appropriate, meek, modest, and self-controlled, bringing honor to God, not attention to herself. This doesn't mean she has a personality by-pass! But she is bridled and under control.

Sadly today women who can be described like that are rare. Instead our culture celebrates irreverent women. It's true to say that in order to make it as a pop star a young woman needs to lose the chaste image. We think of (and pray for) Miley Cyrus and any number of women who had their identities transformed to make it big.

There are at least two reasons for a deficiency of womanly self-control. First, there has been a lack of direction and protection from fathers. Dads play a big part in shaping womanhood in their daughters. For instance, I wrestled with both my children, but not in the same way. My daughter did not want to be body-slammed on the living room floor. My son, however, loved it. I pushed Jake to *be physical* with me and I let Ava *play physically* with me. I wanted Jake to test *his strength to be a protector* and I wanted Ava to *feel my strength and respect masculine protection*. I wanted her strength to be inner reverence, not masculine robustness.

Second, many girls lack teaching and an example from mothers in the home and spiritual mothers in the church.

There is a desperate need for spiritual mothers who know what it looks like to be reverent, who model it for young girls in a way a man cannot and who teach it to other women. My wife has been a model of womanhood for our daughter who has listened to her words and watched her actions over her 19 years. Spiritual mothers like Elisabeth Elliot are the need of the hour. Can girls play with boys growing up? Yes, of course. Can they get dirty in the mud? Yes! But ask yourself, as they grow, are you as a mother cultivating reverence in your daughters through the activities and sports you encourage—an attitude befitting a priestess?

Godly mothers train their daughters in modest ways. In 1 Timothy 2:9-10, Paul says the following of womanly modesty: 'women should adorn themselves in respectable apparel, with modesty and self-control, not with braided hair and gold or pearls or costly attire, but with what is proper for women who profess godliness—with good works.' Reverence is rooted in a fear of the Lord and it issues forth in a modesty of dress and speech. These are strange words in our time, but reverence actually creates a certain style of dress in the apostle's mind.

Note that Paul encourages women to be beautiful and enhance their beauty by what they wear. This is not an excuse for a lack of care in the way they dress. They are to adorn themselves, but the outward apparel is reflecting an inward reverent disposition. So a wife should dress in a way that is attractive to her husband but is not sensuous. There is a great difference between beauty and sensuality. One is holy; the other is sinful.

True womanhood cultivates true beauty. In 1 Peter 3, the apostle says the following: 'Do not let your adorning be external—the braiding of hair and the putting on of gold jewelry, or the clothing you wear, but let your adorning be the hidden person of the heart with the imperishable beauty of a gentle and quiet spirit, which in God's sight is very precious' (1 Pet. 3:3). These words speak to an adorning that is precious in God's sight: a woman clothing herself with a gentle and quiet spirit. How contrary is this vision of adornment to what we commonly see in pop culture.

Paul's words frame not only attitude, but appearance. A woman can be attractive without extravagance. My wife will often say to my daughter, 'Frame the face, not the body. Use make-up but don't do it to draw attention to yourself.' This kind of reverence is a lost posture in womanhood today. A woman's value and worth are not contingent upon what she looks like. Buying into that lie makes young girls have a 'Look at me' attitude, not a 'look at God attitude.' A woman's worth is from God. Physical appearance is second to character and should not be ignored. However, biblical wisdom says, 'Charm is deceitful, and beauty is vain, but a woman who fears the LORD is to be praised' (Prov. 31:30).[10]

A gentle and quiet spirit that pleases God is found only when a woman fears God. When she fears God, she won't fear what others think. She won't compare her looks, body and clothes with other women and lose heart, and she won't compare her looks, body and clothes with other women and grow proud. Fearing the Lord makes her focus on what He prescribes for true beauty. This kind of beauty is imperishable. It is attractive. This kind of womanhood is strong and courageous, for it faces down the lies of Satan and a sinful heart and chooses godliness by the Spirit's power.

Women are called to a posture of deep respect. We think of Eph. 5:33: 'Let the wife see to it that she respects

---

10. See Mary Mohler, *Modeling Modesty* (Louisville: SBTS Press, 2009).

her husband.' Respect is expressed in modesty of dress but also in speech and conduct. That word respect here means 'fear' or reverence for one in authority. Peter corroborates this teaching in 1 Peter 3:1-2: 'Likewise, wives, be subject to your own husbands, so that even if some do not obey the word, they may be won without a word by the conduct of their wives, when they see your respectful and pure conduct.' Wives should fear to disrespect the authority of their husbands firstly because they disrespect God's order. Secondly, if they see their mother disrespecting their father her children will be disrespectful. We recall the warning from the Old Testament: 'A wife who shames him is as rottenness to his bones' (Prov. 12:4). Women are called to take care of how they engage their husbands. The stakes here are high.

What if a wife doesn't feel like respecting her husband? What if he doesn't warrant respect? 1 Peter 3:1-6 is written for the wife of an unbelieving husband who is not a godly leader. Yet she is still called to respect him and to win him with reverence. A wife's respectful submission to her husband is not contingent upon his godly leadership. She never follows him into sin, but she is called to respect him, not because his behavior necessarily deserves it, but because Christ places him as the head and calls her to respect him. She respects her husband's God-given position before she respects his personality or performance: 'the head of every man is Christ, the head of a wife is her husband, and the head of Christ is God' (1 Cor. 11:3). The godly wife submits out of love for Christ.

A key part of this posture is respectful speech. One example of this is found in Sarah's attitude toward her husband, Abraham. She obeyed him 'by calling him lord' (1 Pet. 3:6). Respect or reverence doesn't mean being shy and silent. It means being soft and resolute. It means having one's eyes fixed upon God, and therefore continually working to honor one's head. This attitude takes courage. Ultimately, it can only proceed from the presence of the Spirit in a woman's heart. Rather than feeling entitled to a better husband she is thankful for the one God has given her. Therefore she will look to build him up with her speech. She can disagree with her husband but her tone will be respectful rather than demanding. Think, 'How does God want me to respond to help my husband change?'[11]

Peter continues, 'And you are her children, if you do good and do not fear anything that is frightening' (1 Pet. 3:6). Hope in God drives out frightening things like respecting imperfect authority. If a wife trusts God and His word for womanhood, she can respect what God wisely designs for the sexes and how they interact. As in 1 Corinthians 11:7, the Scripture teaches that a wife brings glory to her husband when she respects his position as her head.

A wife should also take care how she talks to and about her husband publicly. She should take a respectful tone. It is important because God has ordained this for His glory in her. When a wife respects her husband in the way she speaks to him, she shows her children and the world that Christ is a leader worthy of respect. She reflects the way Christ respects the authority of the Father. He never speaks disrespectfully to Him or about Him.

God didn't give a wife a lobotomy when He gave her a husband. She doesn't need to always agree with him to respect him. But there is an attitude to authority that the Lord does

---

11. Martha Peace, *The Excellent Wife: A Biblical Perspective* (Bemidji, MN: Focus, 1995), 113. The chapter, 'Respect', is outstanding.

want her to have. All Christian women must realize that they are that kind of woman: that Proverbs 31, 1 Timothy 2, Titus 2, Ephesians 5, 1 Peter 3 woman.

There is much grace for wives who seek to be respectful but sometimes stumble. Thankfully, Christ's sin-bearing, forgiveness-bringing death covers the failures of the couple. This is deeply encouraging for the godly wife. Savoring the work of Jesus frees her from fear of man and grows in her the fear of God, enabling and empowering her to trust His word for womanhood. Christian women, Scripture teaches, are redeemed not to be rebellious, but to be reverent.

The Response: Submission under Sovereignty

Malcolm in the Middle was a popular TV program in the early 2000s. Malcolm is a genius middle kid in a dysfunctional family where the mum is the authority and the dad is childish. Authority structures in the home are upside down and this is mirrored in the school where bullies rule and teachers are indifferent. Hence the young Malcolm thinks life is unfair and yearns for structure by breaking free of any structure. This is reflected in the refrains of the show's theme tune, 'You're not the boss of me now.' This line epitomizes the lack of submission to authority that we observe in culture. Submission is a dirty word nowadays. We equate it to oppression or perversion (think of *Fifty Shades of Grey*).

As we have seen, however, biblical submission is beautiful. It is a central feature of biblical womanhood. It is vital to understand that a woman's role as a helper, her reverent attitude and her submissive response are tied together in God's sovereign purposes from creation (as we've seen) but also in redemption. The point of this chapter is to say that *the purpose of submission is rooted in the sovereignty of God in salvation.* We know this from two passages in Ephesians. In Ephesians 1:5-7 Paul says, 'In love he predestined us for adoption as sons through Jesus Christ, according to the purpose of his will, *to the praise of his glorious grace,* with which he has blessed us in the Beloved. In him we have redemption through his blood, the forgiveness of our trespasses, according to the riches of his grace.' This means that in eternity past God had a plan to put on display His glory, particularly the glory of His grace, in sending His son to die for sinners (v. 6). So we could say that the gospel is the apex of God's glory. That was God's plan.

Then in Ephesians 5:31, Paul, who has just been talking about husbands and wives and how they are to relate to each other, says: 'Therefore a man shall leave his father and mother and hold fast to his wife, and the two shall become one flesh. This mystery is profound, and I am saying that *it refers to Christ and the church.*' Marriage between a man and a woman is designed to put on display that glory, the glory of the gospel mentioned in Chapter 1:6. The apex of God's glory is the gospel and marriage is a picture of the gospel.

But it is not just marriage in general that is in view, it is marriage involving Christ-like headship of a husband and church-like submission of a wife. So we read in Ephesians 5:22-24. 'Wives, submit to your own husbands, as to the Lord. For the <u>husband</u> is the head of the **wife** even as <u>Christ</u> is the head of the **church**, his body, and is himself its Saviour. Now as the church submits to Christ, so also wives should submit in everything to their husbands.' A wife's submission to her husband's headship portrays the gospel. So the relational order of headship and submission in marriage is no more interchangeable than the relational order of Christ and the church in salvation.

Tamper with the order and you tell a lie about the gospel. In marriage, a wife is to submit to her own husband who is her head in the same way that the church gladly and voluntarily submits to her head, Christ. As Elisabeth Elliot said, 'Submission *is* her strength.'[12] Submission exists to say something about God's sovereign plan of salvation in the gospel. That's huge!

Even as we lay out the glorious design of God in marriage, we should offer a few caveats on submission. A wife should never submit to her husband if he is leading her into sin because Christ is her ultimate head and he is holy. She should not passively accept physical or psychological abuse. In cases of abuse, she should call the police. She should also call her elders, and get out of there. She is not called to submit to abuse. Any abuse of authority is sin and is contrary to Scripture and to the complementarian view of the roles that men and women have within marriage. Abuse is a perversion of authority, not a part of it.[13]

If her husband forbids her to go to church, or prohibits her from ever pointing out his sin or encourages her to participate in sexual immorality, she should respectfully refuse. She can explain that she wants to submit to his leadership but what he is asking of her is contrary to Scripture and her ultimate leader, Jesus Christ. Remember: roles were distorted at the fall, so dysfunction of headship and submission is a result of sin, not the pre-fall divine design.

There are going to be times—let us be honest—when living out this design is hard. Submission can be challenging. We

---

12. Elliot, 93.

13. Point 6 of the Danvers Statement Rationale states that the document was written because of a concern over, 'the upsurge of physical and emotional abuse in the family'. Biblical complementarity is the polar opposite of abuse, and is the chief threat to it. http://cbmw.org/about/danvers-statement/

ourselves as husbands can easily look back and see times when we got things wrong, and made it hard for our wives to follow us. We grieve over this. Further, we feel much empathy for women in hard places, wedded to men who do not lead them or pursue the Lord wholeheartedly. Of course, even the best husband is just a shadow of Christ, and so all godly women must exercise patience as their husbands grow over time.

No husband will lead perfectly, just as no wife will submit perfectly. One of the most persuasive lies Satan whispers to women is that their husband alone gets things wrong, and that if they had a different husband, submission would be easy as pie. But this is not true. Not at all. Every man is fallen; every woman is fallen. God has called us to just the marriage He's given us, and that is the marriage in which we must live our biblical roles.

Women must remember this when the lack of growth and leadership in their husband discourages them. *This is the husband God has given me*, they can say. *He is the one I will seek to honor, follow, and submissively encourage in godliness.* This kind of resolute womanhood is just what Peter identified as evangelistically potent and deeply God-honoring. The payoff for such godliness may not come in this life. Marriages are targeted by Satan and can, if unhappy, foster discouragement. But all who obey the Lord per biblical teaching will be rewarded in the life to come.

If wives feel over-taxed—and all will—they do well to pray much, and to remember that submission to the will of the Father meant the Son going to the cross. There is no higher cost than this. But there was also tremendous glory in Christ's posture. In the times when it is hard to follow a husband's lead, a wife does well to fix her eyes on Christ. In Him, a woman finds her example of perfect submission (Phil. 2:5-11). Through

Him, a biblical woman embraces being a helper, a God-honoring servant with a reverent attitude and a willingness to follow appropriate masculine leadership. This is life-giving, God-exalting womanhood in an age that so desperately needs to rediscover it.

At the heart of godly femininity is beauty, true beauty. Such loveliness is more than appearance; it is much more excellent than charm or talent. You see the beauty of womanhood in the hospital room as a mother brings forth life. You see this beauty in a surprisingly reverent and submissive attitude in a world gone rebellious. You see this beauty in a woman who fearlessly defies Satan and dares to do something truly outrageous in today's world: to live in distinct ways as a woman for the greater glory of God.

CHAPTER FOUR

Complementarity In The Family, Church and Culture

In J. R. R. Tolkien's essay 'On Fairy-Stories' he speaks of the power of story to reveal hidden worlds.

> In its fairy tale or other world setting, it is a sudden and miraculous grace, never to be counted on to reoccur. It does not deny the existence of dyscatastrophe, or sorrow and failure, the possibility of these is necessary to the joy of deliverance. It denies, (in the face of much evidence if you will) universal final defeat and insofar is evangelium,

> giving a fleeting glimpse of Joy, Joy beyond the walls
> of the world, poignant as grief.[1]

To put it another way, the fairy tale gives us a glimpse of joy in another world. We resonate with this narratival power as believers. Christians, after all, are 'new creations' (2 Cor. 5:17), sojourners (1 Pet. 2:11) and citizens of heaven (Phil. 3:20). We live with our feet on the ground, but our very lives provide a glimpse of the good life, of true joy found in a new world and another culture.

In what follows, we will show how obeying God's design for men and women gives others a window into this otherworldly society. Here is our outline:

1. Love And Order In The Trinity
2. Love And Order In The Home
3. Love And Order In The Church
4. The Battle For Love And Order In A Loveless And Disordered World

1. Love And Order In the Trinity

First, the perfect world is designed by the perfect architect. *God* is the divine architect, the maker of men and women and this world (Gen. 1:1). In other words, there is an uncreated God and He designs and creates everything else. Second, we see that in this world there is perfect community. The triune God has eternally existed in perfect community, one of diversity and unity. And He reflects this diverse yet united community by creating man, male and female (Gen. 1:27). Third, within this community there is *love* and *order*. Order

---

1. J. R. R. Tolkien, 'On Fairy-Stories,' in *Essays Presented to Charles Williams*, ed. C. S. Lewis (Grand Rapids: Eerdmans, 1966), 81.

is the way God expresses His love (i) in the relationships of the Trinity, (ii) in an ordered creation, (iii) in a reordering through redemption, and (iv) in the future consummation. Love is expressed through order. God is love (1 John 4:8) and God is a God of order (1 Cor. 14:33).

Let me explain further. The Trinity is a relationship of love. The Father loves the Son (John 3:35; 5:20), the Son loves the Father (John 14:31), and the Spirit is the love of God conveyed to us (Rom. 5:5). John Piper puts it so well: 'The Son is the eternal image that the Father has of his own perfections, and the Holy Spirit is the eternal love that flows between the Father and the Son as they delight in each other.'[2] This relationship of love is expressed through relationships of authority and submission. There is order. The Father is the Father because He sends the Son. The Son is the Son because He submits to the Father's will. The Spirit is the Spirit because the Father and the Son send Him. There is no Holy Trinity without the order of authority and submission.

Only through love will order be embraced but only through order will love be expressed. So the perfect world is a world of love and order. In contrast, the imperfect world in which we live is full of hate and disorder. This is the fallen world out of which Christians have been saved and transferred to the kingdom of the beloved Son (Col 1:13). So redeemed men and women can now live out transformed masculinity and femininity, which was God's grand design in the perfect world, in the beginning, to reflect His glory (Isa. 43:6-7). By embracing God's design for manhood and womanhood, Christian men and women in the home, church

2. John Piper, *A Godward Life: Savoring the Supremacy of God in All of Life* (Multnomah Publishers, 1997), 74.

and society give the world a glimpse of love and order. So let's look at the home.

2. Love And Order In The Home

Marriage

When questioned by the Pharisees about divorce, Jesus immediately referred to the Scriptures and to marriage in God's created order.

> He answered, 'Have you not read that he who created them from the beginning made them male and female, and said, "Therefore a man shall leave his father and his mother and hold fast to his wife, and the two shall become one flesh"? So they are no longer two but one flesh. What therefore God has joined together, let not man separate' (Matt. 19:4-6).

Marriage is under attack in our day like never before. In June 2015 the United States Supreme Court ruled in favor of the nationwide legalization of same-sex marriage.[3] However, despite that decision and despite a culture which is redefining what it means to be male, female or married, the Bible's view of marriage remains unchanged: God designed marriage as one man and one woman in committed covenant for life, not two men or two women or one man with many women or one woman with many men (Gen. 2:24; Eph. 5). This was Jesus' view and His foundation texts for marriage were Genesis 1:27 and Genesis 2:24.

I recently officiated at the wedding ceremony of my son, Jake, and his bride, Christa. When it came to the vows he

---

3. See CBMW's 'Official Response to the SCOTUS Ruling,' June 26, 2015, accessible at http://cbmw.org/topics/homosexuality/cbmws-official-response-to-the-scotus-ruling.

promised to honor and *'cherish'* her and she promised to honor and *'obey'* him. By their vows they wanted to embrace the beauty of manhood and womanhood and to delineate the God-ordained difference in their roles. He will love and cherish her and she will respect and submit to him.

The lines for marriage are drawn in 1 Corinthians 11. Husbands are called to exercise leadership over their wives patterned after Trinitarian order (God the Father's authority over the Son): God –> Christ –> Husband –> Wife (1 Cor. 11:3). A husband also exercises this headship due to creation order: the woman was made from the man (1 Cor. 11:8-9), thus giving the man primacy of leadership in the Garden as he names her 'woman' and 'Eve' (Gen. 2:23; 3:20).

In addition to Trinitarian and creation foundations, a husband's marital leadership finds its pattern in the redemption order: Christ's headship over the church and its submission to Him (Eph. 5:22). Therefore, headship has Trinitarian, creational, and redemptive meaning. Finally, marriage finds its goal when Jesus the Bridegroom, consummates the marriage by taking His Bride, the church, forever (Rev. 19:7-8).

A wife submits to her husband's leadership primarily *because of his divinely appointed position.* This is crucial to understand. Her submission owes first to his position, not to his capability. Counter-cultural as this may be, submission is not based on competency or rights but on God's grand design. Marriage between one man and one woman, created in the image of the triune God, is a picture of redemption with its goal in consummation.

We need to see how men and women are swept up in this grand design. In our egalitarian age, there is a great need for husbands to recover confidence in the design and to exercise real leadership in the marriage. And wives must recover that same confidence in order to encourage and receive this leadership. Men should not apologize for being in charge in the relationship. Man was created to exercise lordship with Adam as head (Gen. 1:28-30; Gen. 2:15-17). This involves taking benevolent rule and subduing creation. This is also the case in the marriage:

> Wives, submit to your own husbands, as to the Lord. For the husband is the head of the wife even as Christ is the head of the church, his body, and is himself its Savior. Now as the church submits to Christ, so also wives should submit in everything to their husbands (Eph. 5:22-24).

As we see in this passage, marriage gives the world a glimpse into God's original design to display His glory through a man and woman in a one-flesh covenant, the fruit of which was to be the multiplication of this glory through the multiplication of His image bearers (Gen. 1:26-18; Gen. 2:24). Moreover, in Ephesians 5 Paul makes clear the ultimate purpose of marriage with this stunning statement, 'Therefore a man shall leave his father and mother and hold fast to his wife, and the two shall become one flesh. This mystery is profound, and I am saying that *it refers to Christ and the church.*'

We are reminded of how the Puritans used to refer to marriage as a vocation. It was a calling from God to be a husband or wife and everything served God's purposes within the marriage: headship, submission, sex, and children. The Puritans' 'passion to please God expressed itself in an ardor for order.'[4] This God-centered vision orients a husband and

---

4. J. I. Packer, from his chapter 'Marriage and the Family in Puritan Thought', *A Quest For Godliness: The Puritan Vision of the Christian Life* (Wheaton: Crossway, 1990), 272.

wife to the fact their marriage doesn't belong to them in order to serve their purposes. Marriage is for God. A wife is called to be subject to her husband 'as to the Lord' (Eph. 5:23) and 'in everything' (Eph. 5:24) just as the church submits to Christ. Wives must submit to their own husbands with a church-like responsiveness by honoring his Christ-like leadership. The roles of husbands and wives are not interchangeable because the roles of the Bridegroom, Christ, and His Bride, the Church are not interchangeable. The roles are packed with meaning and purpose.

A wife should submit to her own husband 'in everything.' This doesn't mean mindless servitude to everything her husband says. She is a member of the church the same as him (1 Pet. 3:6) and her ultimate submission is to Christ who is the ultimate head of the church (Col. 1:18). Rather, submission involves an inner attitude, not just an outward agreement. At the end of this passage, in Ephesians 5:33 this attitude is described as 'respect.' She should have the inclination to respond to and affirm and encourage her husband's leadership in all aspects of their life together.

This has special relevance to decision-making. A husband's headship means that he is primarily responsible for deciding on a biblical plan for his family. This doesn't mean that he decides on everything but he should initiate as a pattern in the marriage. And if he is a wise head he will solicit his wife's counsel in these things. Her wisdom is priceless because she knows him better than anyone else and she is made to be a helper for him. He should encourage her help.

So if my wife has reservations about a plan I put forward (let's say moving from the UK to Canada!) that should be an immediate red flag for me. I want to give time to hear her wisdom. So where I can put off making that decision I will. We will go away, search the Scriptures, think and pray about it before we revisit the discussion. My aim, as leader, is consensus. I don't want to drag my wife where she does not want to go. This is not about my making the decision but my leading her in *our* making a decision as one.

However, if a decision must be made and we are both in deadlock, then I am responsible before God to make that decision: rather than it being my right, it is my responsibility. If it proves me correct I don't lord it over Amanda, and if I am wrong, I take the blame and protect her from the consequences. Remember Christ does not coerce the church. He woos the church and loves her by laying His life down for her that He may win her heart and her glad obedience. His authority is not harsh and manipulative but loving and winsome. But remember He takes the initiative, according to God's plan, for the church's good and the glory of the Father.

Once a decision or plan is made a wife is called to help her husband put that plan into action. Her husband might delegate much authority so that she can help him execute the plan. But this oversight is not independent of him. The husband shouldn't micro-manage but he must oversee. Equally his authority is not independent of her because it is exercised towards her for her good. Remember, a qualification of an elder (overseer) is to 'manage' his household well (1 Tim. 3:4).

The heartbeat of this management involves lovingly leading his wife in decision-making. It extends also to biblical study. Ephesians 5:25-27 calls for this sort of practice on the husband's part:

> Husbands, love your wives, as Christ loved the church and gave himself up for her, that he might

sanctify her, having cleansed her *by the washing of water with the word*, so that he might present the church to himself in splendor, without spot or wrinkle or any such thing, that she might be holy and without blemish.

It is Jesus who sanctifies our wives. We cannot do this work on our own terms. But in imitation of Christ's leadership, we seek to cultivate the heart of our wife.[5] We open up Scripture with her and share wisdom from it with her. We do so not as an overbearing professor, but as a loving husband seeking to be like Christ, bringing the Word to our wives.

If the model for a husband is Christ's sacrificial love for the church, then His goal must be the pattern also. Christ's goal is that the church will be 'without spot or wrinkle or any such thing' and 'holy and without blemish.' She will be a holy bride fit for a holy bridegroom. Holiness will characterize her. Because a husband models his love on Christ's love, he seeks to strengthen her spiritually. This means opening the Word of God with her. It means discussing it with her and building her up in it. So says John Piper:

> Gather your wife and children for family devotions everyday—call it whatever you want: family prayers, family worship, family Bible time. Take the initiative to gather them. If you don't know what to do, ask some brothers what they do. Or ask your wife what she would like to do. You don't have to be a loner here. Remember, headship takes primary responsibility, not sole responsibility. The wife, we pray, is always supporting and helping. And regularly has gifts that

---

5. Chanski, *Manly Dominion*, 137.

> the husband doesn't. What women rightly long for is spiritual and moral initiative, from a man, not spiritual and moral domination.[6]

We need these practices today. Unfortunately, many of us fall short in this respect. Some husbands are great physical protectors and providers. There is food on the table and a roof over his wife's head, and he would never let anyone touch her. But when it comes to spiritual protection and provision he fails. Yet this is a primary means of her growth and a primary way that he loves her.

We men often abdicate this responsibility because of fear, laziness or insensitivity. Some of us fear inadequacy—a man's wife may be more theologically educated than he. Others fear the responsibility. Some of us are simply too lazy to do the hard work of planning and carrying through on the moral trajectory in the home. Others fail because they are insensitive to their wife's needs. They drown her with a dissertation on predestination instead of washing her gently with a word in season.[7]

We cannot forget that our headship issues forth in spiritual protection grounded in love. This means that we step up and lead in various ways—even correcting false thinking if necessary. Adam's mistake, we recall, was that

---

6. John Piper, 'Lionhearted and Lamblike: The Christian Husband as Head, Part 2: What Does It Mean to Lead?,' accessible at http://www.desiringgod. org/messages/lionhearted-and-lamblike-the-christian-husband-as-head-part-2. In published form, see John Piper, *This Momentary Marriage: A Parable of Permanence* (Wheaton, IL: Crossway, 2009).

7. Thoughtful perspectives on a husband's ministry to his wife include, Eric Mason, *Manhood Restored: How The Gospel Makes Men Whole* (B&H Publishing, 2013), 133-136. Also see Richard D. Phillips, *The Masculine Mandate: God's Calling to Men* (Reformation Trust Publishing, 2010), 83-87.

he did not correct his wife when she was getting God's word wrong in Eden. He did not love Eve by failing in this regard. His abdication of spiritual and theological leadership was profoundly unloving, and so is ours.

Even if we struggle, the Lord will give us grace to lead our wives and children. We do not need to be biblical experts, praise God. Any man of God can lead his wife and family spiritually. His spiritual care for his household begins with his personal time in the Word and prayer. He can be like the miner in Job 28. He must go down into God's word for wisdom and come up with a nugget, not just for himself but also for his wife. Beyond the husband-wife dynamic, in family devotions, he solicits his wife's thoughts, offers thoughts for reflection and, if necessary, correction, and prays. This should be a warm and happy time, not a rigid and chilly one. We want devotions to be joyful, not interminable.[8]

A wife is not prohibited from pointing out her husband's sin, either (Gal. 6:1). She must do so, in fact. But there will be a respectful way she does this, rather than aggressively confronting him or nagging him, which might drive him to frustration (Prov. 21:9).[9] If a woman of God, she has the Holy Spirit, and she has wisdom that he not only will profit from, but that he needs. Further, she knows his weaknesses better than anyone else, and so in respectful and discreet ways helps him grow by bringing them to light.

Godly men do not turn away from such conviction. They welcome it as the gift of God to them, and they seek to program

---

8. See the excellent practical guide to family worship by Don Whitney, *Family Worship: In the Bible, in History & in Your Home* (2006); the fuller version is Whitney, *Family Worship* (Wheaton: Crossway, 2016).

9. Peace, *The Excellent Wife*, 142-44. Martha has a very helpful section here on how a wife can reprove her husband respectfully.

opportunities for their wives to speak into their lives. Too many Christian women have no forum to air their concerns, and so frustration understandably rises to a boil like water in a kettle. In the interest of marital harmony and humble leadership, men can lead the couple in a weekly conversation when both spouses exchange both encouragement and gracious critique. Such leadership speaks well of a man. The godliest men are those who not only help their wives understand the Bible and its doctrine, but those who create opportunities for their own sin to be exposed and repented of.

In sum, a wife is not mute as her husband opens up the Word with her. She participates, shares her thoughts, asks questions, and experiences blessing—ideally—as her husband sets time aside to study Scripture with her and thus exercises Christlike leadership in the home. A wife can encourage her husband in this. Words like, 'I love it when you lead me with God's Word' or a simple 'Thank you' augment a man's resolve to press on in leading his family to know the Word. As he undertakes this work, he connects his own time with the Lord to their time as a couple with the Lord. My wife Amanda and I have seen great blessing in this.

Men are called by Paul in Ephesians 5 to nourish and cherish their wife as their own body (Eph. 5:29). How could a man who would feed and clothe his body not do the same for his wife? She is in one-flesh union with him (Eph. 5:28-31). The connection is profound and yet again mirrors Christ and the church that is His body. Too many times a man will pray for his wife and ask God to help her with her problems without a single thought to the fact that her problems are his problems. She is his body. He is the protection that God has provided.

This entails a self-denying, others-centered posture. He must live with his wife in an understanding way, he must listen to her, and he must know what God requires of him as a husband and her as a wife (1 Pet. 3:7). Then he must act accordingly. There is a warning in 1 Peter 3:7. A husband's prayers will 'not be answered' if he doesn't obey. First, this reminds us that he is a man in authority but in submission to the one true authority. Second, he must exercise leadership as God prescribes.

It might be that he needs to simply hold his wife and comfort her with a word of assurance. It might be that he needs to insert a word of authority into her life and relieve her of one too many burdens that she has taken on. This is love. This is cultivating a wife's heart. This releases a wife to be the helper she needs to be. But it is amazing how many men will not do it and how many women will refuse it.

In a marriage, headship and submission look like love and respect. But this takes self-denial on both parts. A husband humbly dies to his preferences and his sin and he loves his wife. A wife humbly dies to her preferences and sin and she respects her husband. Of course a husband should respect his wife (1 Pet. 3:7) and a wife should love her husband (Titus 2:4). But God wants sacrificial love to mark manhood and respect to mark womanhood. As each spouse fulfills their role, they bring out the God-appointed purpose in the other.

In the providence of God, a man and wife are often strong in areas where the other is weak. No man and woman are perfectly compatible, because perfect compatibility would mean there was never a need to extend grace, patience and forgiveness. How can unconditional love be shown if the person meets all the conditions? Unconditional love takes an other-centered perspective. It means death to self. Jesus, without grasping at equality to the Father, humbly obeyed

His divine head even to death on a cross (Phil. 2:5-11). Christ's death to self not only saved men and women but also provides the template for love and respect in a marriage.

This means a man loving his wife so that he willingly prefers her good to the ball game or the hobby or the study. He acts practically on Ephesians 5:33, which says the following to couples: 'let each one of you love his wife as himself, and let the wife see that she respects her husband.' This also means a wife laying aside her ambitions to prefer her husband's goals and to help him achieve them. It means both of them making one another their first ministry even when children come along. It means humility and sacrifice for both parties.

This kind of marriage speaks a better word about God, manhood and womanhood and it shows a better world to the surrounding culture. It gives a present glimpse of a better world to come: one where the meaning of marriage will be a heavenly reality as the Bridegroom takes His Bride, and in 'fairy tale' language, they really do live happily ever after in the new heaven and the new earth (Rev. 21:11).

Parenting

> Children, obey your parents in the Lord, for this is right. Honor your father and mother (this is the first commandment with a promise), that it may go well with you and that you may live long in the land. Fathers, do not provoke your children to anger, but bring them up in the discipline and instruction of the Lord (Eph. 6:1-4).

One of the big reasons why marriage is the foundation for a flourishing society is its unique designation to produce children through the union of one man and one woman.[10] Of course, making Christians is a work of God by regeneration, not procreation (John 1:13; 3:1-8), but a Christian marriage exposes children to a gospel environment. Parents provide a culture in the home that is different than the world.

Children get to hear gospel words and experience gospel transformation in their parents' lives. This means that parents cannot make the children the center of the home. Children should come into the home and fit under the authority of the central relationship of husband and wife. It is vital that parents are the leaders, not the children, because parents represent the authority of God to their children.

Again the structure of love and order in building a godly home is extended to the children. Both parents are the authority over the children: we think of 'children obey your parents' alongside 'honor your father and mother' (Col. 3:20; Exod. 20:12). Even in the past year, Premier League football manager Tony Pulis spoke on BBC radio about the great need for mentoring in football today. He noted that apprentices nowadays were undisciplined and lack self-control. He put it down to the breakdown of the family and absent father figures in the lives of young men. But he did cite Christian family values as one thing that had a good effect.

Both parents should be obeyed and of one mind in their child rearing (Prov. 1:8). Children are masterminds at playing one parent off against another. This can cause disunity between the parents and disunited leadership is no leadership at all. From a young age a child can learn that it will go well with them if they obey their parents and it won't go well for them if they don't.

---

10. Adapted from Gavin Peacock, 'David's Succession: Lessons for Fathers,' in Jeff Jones, ed., *Shadows of the King: Pastoral Meditations on the Book of First Kings* (Calgary: Calvary Grace Church, 2015), 19-24.

Where men have been emasculated or men are absent, and where manhood has lost its distinctiveness, biblical fathering is something of the past. All the following points are applicable to mothers, but Paul's instruction to fathers in Ephesians 6:4 makes clear that fathers must lead in discipline.[11]

A father's discipline

David's regular failure to discipline his children is highlighted in First Kings 1:6. Speaking with reference to Adonijah, the author says: 'His father had never at any time displeased him by asking, "Why have you done thus and so?"' (1 Kings 1:6). David indulged Adonijah. He sinned by omission in not correcting him and training him. The result was a spoiled and disobedient son who eventually turned into an entitled young man.

Acting early prevents ruinous consequences later because a child left undisciplined today will become the bane of society tomorrow. When he exercises justice, a father shows care for the child he disciplines, and (if it is the case) for the one his child sins against. However, too often fathers are afraid to 'displease' their children: they are afraid of pushback, or a bad reaction. Especially with teenagers there is often a fear that they will run away or indulge further in sin if a father imposes correction and restrictions.

---

11. P. T. O'Brien notes that '"oi pateres" can denote "parents" in general (Heb. 11:23; cf. W. Bauer, W. F. Ardnt, F. W. Gingrich and F. W. Danker, *Greek-English Lexicon of the New Testament*(2nd ed.) 635), but there is a change of wording in v. 4 (from goneis, "parents", in v. 1), suggesting that "oi pateres" means "fathers", while there is no mention of mothers after the explicit reference to them in the commandment of v. 2. Further, in the ancient world, in both Graeco-Roman and Jewish writings, fathers were responsible for the education of their children.' *The Pillar New Testament Commentary: The Letter To The Ephesians* (Grand Rapids: Eerdmans, 1999), 445.

Ultimately, a father who doesn't discipline is seeking his own comfort. In that case, the father has forgotten his responsibility as head of the home and as the primary authority over his children. But too often the authority structure is reversed. Discipline sometimes requires spanking, but it always involves training and correction. 'Folly is bound up in the heart of a child, but the rod of discipline drives it far from him' (Prov. 22:15).

Fathers who coddle their children and will not exercise biblically-mandated authority sin by their omission, and do harm to their children and others through them. This may also provoke their children to anger and resentment through their lack of loving correction. A man who says, 'I'm a softie—I could never spank my disobedient child' is, without knowing it, robbing his children of essential spiritual formation. Though he thinks he is being loving, he is actually being cruel, for children need to learn obedience (Exod. 20:12; Deut. 6:4-9; Prov. 13:24). To be taught to obey in a loving home is a gracious gift of the Father who Himself must be obeyed as an expression of love (1 John 5:3).

Nevertheless, fathers must discipline with the right attitude—not being harsh or domineering, which will provoke children to anger (Eph. 6:4). In other words, the impatient, self-serving, severe father can cause a child to become disheartened. Fathers must discipline their children by dealing with the heart issue behind their sin. They should direct their children towards what pleases the Lord, not simply their father or mother. They must display the displeasure of God (He is holy and hates sin) and the mercy of God (He is merciful and offers forgiveness). This way a father shepherds his child's heart and directs it towards the grace of the cross of Christ. Behaviour modification is superficial.

In sum, discipline should be consistent, loving, and wise. This is true of both parents: a Christian mother's teaching is kindness to be received and wisdom to be heeded (Prov. 31:26). Nevertheless, as we are at pains to say, fathers have a unique role as head of the household to lead in the discipline and instruction of their children (Eph. 6:4). A godly father uniquely displays the Fatherhood of God (Heb. 12).

So much of a father's work is heart-work in order to produce repentance and faith in his children. In his autobiography, John G. Paton tells of his father's loving discipline. With serious issues he would go to private prayer. Paton recalls, '…we boys got to understand that he was laying the whole matter before God; and that was the severest punishment for me to bear… We loved him all the more when we saw how much it cost him to punish us…we were ruled by love far more than by fear.'[12] Fathers, let us discipline our children with that attitude.

A father's teaching

Fathers should also start teaching their charges early. David taught Solomon from a 'tender' age (Prov. 4:3). There is a time when the spirit of a child is most flexible and that is when they are young. Character building in the early years is far easier than later on when bad habits are ingrained. Both a mother and father teach their children but it is a father's responsibility to lead in family devotions and overall direction.

The aim of a father's teaching, as with discipline, is that his children would love and obey God. David says to Solomon:

> Be strong, and show yourself a man, and keep the charge of the LORD your God, walking in his ways

---

12. John G. Paton, *Missionary Patriarch: The True Story of John G. Paton*, ed. James Paton (San Antonio: The Vision Forum, 2002-7), 17.

and keeping his statutes, his commandments, his
rules, and his testimonies, as it is written in the Law
of Moses (1 Kings 2:2-3).

Instruction must always be done in the context of commitment
to God's ways and words. Remember Paul tells fathers to
bring their children up in 'the discipline and instruction of
the Lord' (Eph. 6:4). He has Christian teaching in view. And
part of this responsibility is teaching biblical masculinity
and femininity. David's final words to his son, Solomon,
are distinctly masculine. He says, 'show yourself a man'
(1 Kings 2:2). That means there is particular manly behaviour,
which is different from that of a woman.

David unpacks this as leadership involving sacrificial
provision and protection for the sons of Barzillai, and exacting
justice upon Joab and Shimei (1 Kings 2:5-9). So, teaching
children to love and obey God means teaching them to be a
biblical man or woman.

A father's example
Nevertheless, fathers must also *be* what they teach their
children. Otherwise, a child will see a hypocrite. Paul, a
spiritual father to many, says many times, 'Imitate me' (cf.
1 Cor. 4:16; 11:1). In other words, 'Don't just say what I say,
do what I do, be like me.' Children will follow what they see
in their father's life as much as what they hear from their
father's mouth. So there should be no gap between his life and
doctrine. Integrity of character is king because he must not
only teach his children what to do, but he must show them
how it's done. And the way a father treats their mother will
speak volumes to his children about manhood, womanhood,
marriage and Christ.

This kind of family becomes a witness to others in the neighbourhood. It becomes a place where the children's friends will see a different world; a world without confusion of the sexes; a world where a husband loves his wife and a wife respects her husband; a world where children are lovingly cared for, taught and disciplined and where they obey their parents; a world of love and order with Christ at the centre.

However, the bigger and eternal family is the church, which includes men and women, married, singles, orphans and widows. This is the only society that will continue. While human marriage is a picture of the gospel, and the family presents a gospel environment, the church is the new humanity that the gospel creates. It is in the church that the world truly sees the fullest glimpse of a foretaste of heaven. And so we move from the home to the household of God.

3. Love And Order In The Church

A household

> I hope to come to you soon, but I am writing these things to you so that, if I delay, you may know how one ought to behave in the household of God, which is the church of the living God, a pillar and buttress of the truth (1 Tim. 3:14-15).

In this stirring passage, Paul refers to the church as a family—the household of God. In other places he points to its familial relationships: mothers, fathers, brothers, sisters (1 Tim. 5:1-2). The design of the nuclear home is correlated to the household of God. So, as in the home there will be an order of roles within the church family. In the church male elders exercise authority and loving oversight. The elder is a 'husband of one wife' (1 Tim. 3: 2). He need not be married but he must be a man who is faithful to his wife if he is married. He must also manage his household well or it disqualifies him from managing the household of God (1 Tim. 3:4).

The same masculine character of leadership is required for both. In many ways the elders are with the congregation in a husband-wife relationship. The complementary order of authority and submission patterned in the family of the Trinity and marriage and the home is also evident in the church family.

Male leadership

> I do not permit a woman to teach or to exercise authority over a man; rather, she is to remain quiet (1 Tim. 2:12).

This text has been taken numerous ways, many of which the Apostle Paul himself would not recognise. Some people want to dismiss this command because they say Paul was speaking to a unique historical situation of that time not ours, or that the words employed in the text have a different meaning than 'authoritative doctrinal instruction.'[13] Despite the fracas over this verse, it speaks to the responsibility of men to teach and exercise authority in the church. In other words, it prescribes that men carry out the *functions* of teaching and oversight.

This means that women are not permitted to teach a mixed group within the church. It is not simply the *office* of pastor/elder that they cannot hold. Women are called to a much broader application. By the wise mind of God, and according to the order of creation explained in 1 Timothy 2:13, women are not summoned to teach men. They are instructed by God to place themselves under men, and be taught and led

---

13. See Douglas Moo's essay, 'What Does It Mean Not To Teach Or Have Authority Over Men?,' *Recovering Biblical Manhood And Womanhood*, eds. John Piper and Wayne Grudem (Wheaton: Crossway, 1991), 184-188.

by them. 'For Adam was formed first, then Eve; and Adam was not deceived, but the woman was deceived and became a transgressor' (1 Tim. 2:13). This is not a temporary command, which is culturally conditioned; it is God's universal will for the church in every age. It is rooted in God's grand design for men and women from the beginning: Adam as leader, Eve as helper. This principle applies in ways great and small, and does not leave room for elders to approve of women speaking to mixed adult groups, whether for a one-time event or an ongoing series.

We know that some will disagree here in the outworking of this passage. But it is crucial to understand that this portion of Scripture isolates function, not office, as that which conditions the command of God. As a matter of biblical fidelity, though women have ample opportunities to serve and teach in the life of the congregation (see Chapters 3 and 6), women do not teach men. To do so is to stray from biblical wisdom. There is no way around this ancient-sounding reality. Redemption in Christ does not nullify God's pre-fall divine design. There is no new revelation here, and no other word of Scripture contradicts or norms this passage. This is holy and good teaching, and we can only receive it as such. We remember that we prove our trust in God not merely by assenting to the popular parts of the Bible, but the whole counsel of God, challenging as it can be to our fallen sensibilities.

Note that this passage is not indicating that women are more gullible than men (contra wrong readings of 1 Tim. 2:14). Both men and women can be gullible. Remember Samson and how he was duped by Delilah? The flow of 1 Timothy 2:8-13 has been about order in the church. Paul points to the serpent's attack at the fall in Genesis 3 and the usurping and reversal of God's order. Adam was the head. The serpent deliberately approached Eve first instead of Adam. Adam was passive and Eve led Adam.

So we see that the relational order of masculinity and femininity lie at the heart of the fall. From creation it was clear that men should take the lead in the household. From the fall it is clear that disobedience to divine patterns is sinful and puts men and women in danger. In the same way that a husband's headship is for the protection and flourishing of his wife, the church's protection and flourishing rely upon godly male leadership. They are God-appointed shepherds who feed and lead God's flock (1 Peter 5:1-4, cf. Acts 20:28).

And so a healthy church creates a culture of masculine mentorship out of which future elders will emerge. At Calvary Grace we have layers of training: general biblical manhood teaching, one-to-one men mentoring men, leadership opportunities for 'men to watch', involving travel and personal time with an elder and an internship program for men we are considering inviting on as elders. In this way we attempt to develop men of godly faithful character who are apt to teach (the 2 Tim. 2:2 mandate). We also have Titus 2 women's ministry where mature women teach other women. Only a woman knows what it means first-hand to submit to her husband, be a mother, and manage a home.[14]

The egalitarian impulse

In his book, *Manly Dominion*, Mark Chanski, says, 'As flouride is everywhere in the water today, feminism is everywhere in the air today.'[15] I agree with him and would add that there is an unbiblical instinct in our thinking today that is perhaps more prevalent and causing more confusion than we realize.

---

14. Colin Marshall and Tony Payne have articulated this well in their chapter, 'People Worth Watching', *The Trellis and The Vine* (Sydney: Matthias Media, 2009), 127-142.

15. Chanksi, *Manly Dominion*, 167.

In response to 1 Timothy 2:12-14, some wonder whether women can do anything meaningful in the church. At times, this question proceeds from frustration, from the perception that the Bible puts women at a disadvantage. Because of the fall, we all carry within us what we could call an *egalitarian impulse*. This means that we all—in some way—push against God's good design.

Though we might not be aware of it, perhaps, this mentality falls prey to the gender-blurring impulse of our secular age. Unless everything is the same, and everyone fills the same role, we're told, things are fundamentally unjust. We're in an age, after all, when people push for the rights of a girl to play on a boys' sports team and vice versa; when schools open up washrooms of the opposite sex to children who identify as transgender; when public universities demand that the campus community do away with male and female pronouns, or the words 'father' and 'mother', and be called *ze* or *zir*. We can all acknowledge gray areas in our theology, of course. But we must be wary of the drive to blur the lines between the sexes in both identity and role.

The need to develop godly women for ministry is not new. It is ancient. If a church is not growing biblical women, it needs to repent and obey the Scriptures; for Titus 2 is clear about the great need for older women to teach the younger. We need—we *must* have—spiritual mothers in our churches. But the apostolic instruction is for older women to come alongside younger women and teach the core of biblical womanhood: homemaking, loving and submitting to husbands, modeling reverent feminine character (Titus 2:3-5).[16] Women's ministries

---

16. Susan Hunt says, 'When women join together to "perform their proper duties" as corporate helpers and life-givers in the family of God, they contribute to the firmness and stability of the Church,' J. Ligon Duncan & Susan Hunt, *Women's Ministry in the Local Church* (Crossway 2006), 35.

need not fear theology or shy away from it; biblical truth is a gift to all God's people. But we also need to take care to prioritize the teaching role of the elders, those whom God has appointed to exercise theological watch-care over the flock.

In all this, we recognize that owning our God-given role is not easy. It does sometimes feel inequitable. We understand that, and again, this impulse is not new. It was Elizabeth Elliot who said some years ago, 'To accept limitation requires maturity. The child has not yet learned that it cannot have everything. What it sees it wants. What it does not get it screams for. It has to grow up to realize that saying Yes to happiness often means saying No to yourself.'[17] Elliot's words are well-taken. We remember that Eve did not accept her limitations in the garden, even as Adam abdicated his own responsibilities in that same realm. Against their sinful actions, we seek a humble heart that places God's wisdom above its own. It trusts that when He says 'no' that is as gloriously good for us as when He says 'yes.'

These comments apply equally to men's and women's ministries. In the bigger and everlasting family (household) of the church we all relate to each other as brothers and sisters meaning that gender-specific behavior is relevant. When we train men and women in same-sex settings, we help them understand better the very nature of manhood and womanhood. We call men to lead like Christ and we call women to respect and trust like the purified church (Eph. 5:22-33).[18]

---

17. Elisabeth Elliot, *Let Me Be A Woman* (Wheaton: Tyndale, 1976), 63.

18. Andreas & Margaret Kostenberger, *God's Design for Man and Woman: A Biblical-Theological Survey* (Wheaton: Crossway, 2014), 288. This vision for men's and women's ministries with particular focus on teaching manhood and womanhood and yet envisioned under the umbrella of the church family is well put by the Kostenbergers.

We take trouble not only to establish biblical foundations for this behavior, but to guide those under our care to figure out what these great truths mean at a practical level.

The aim of this book is to fill hearts and minds with a thrilling view of manhood and womanhood so that instead of saying in defeated and apologetic tones, 'How far do we have to go with complementarianism in the church?,' people instead say with glad hearts, 'How clearly can we delineate complementarianism in the church to the glory of our great God?' Let's happily affirm the equality but joyfully delineate the difference, celebrating both as the Lord's handiwork.

We have already seen that complementarity begins in the Godhead, is mirrored in creation and finds its pattern and goal in redemption and consummation. On the basis of these deep truths, Christian men and women must show that biblical love and order in the home and the church are not only right, but also that they are gloriously good and we love them.

4. The Battle For Love And Order In A Loveless And Disordered World

As we have already said, the church is the only culture that will last (Rev. 21:1-2). So when biblical men and women step into the workplace and surrounding culture they stand forth as a compelling counter-culture *through their masculinity and femininity.* They give glimpses of glory from another world. The gospel that saves the church is the gospel the church brilliantly portrays to the world. In an age where sexuality is so blurred, biblical manhood and womanhood and marriage are integral to the design of God. Each shines brightly with His glory (Matt. 5:16). But the world, the flesh, and the devil go against God's glory. So there will be a battle to hold the lines of complementarity.

A battle rages

The challenge for any Christian in any age is the battle for the authority of God's Word. Speaking about Martin Luther and his confrontation with culture about the key issues of his day, Elizabeth Rundle Charles wrote these rousing words:

> It is the truth which is assailed in any age which tests our fidelity. It is to confess we are called, not merely to profess. If I profess, with the loudest voice and the clearest exposition, every portion of the truth of God except precisely that little point which the world and the devil are at that moment attacking, I am not confessing Christ, however boldly I may be professing Christianity. Where the battle rages the loyalty of the soldier is proved; and to be steady on all the battle-field besides is mere flight and disgrace to him if he flinches at that one point.[19]

Charles is right. To apply her crucial insight today, biblical sexuality is where the battle for the authority of the Word of God is raging in our culture. It is the bite point. The bite point (as Tim Chester has articulated) is where the gospel challenges the culture and offers truth and calls for repentance.[20] So the church cannot simply *profess* Christ but must *confess* Christ as Lord.

Manhood and womanhood are not limited to the home and church because they are not states you can switch off when you step into in a secular world. And yet it is directly by

---

19. E. R. Charles, *The Chronicles of the Schoenberg Cotta Family* (London: Thomas Nelson, 1864).

20. Tim Chester, 'Planting Biblically Rooted Churches,' November 11, 2013, accessible at https://timchester.wordpress.com/2012/11/13/planting-biblically-rooted-churches.

your adherence to biblical complementarity that you will be different from the world (Rom. 12:2). When people observe a husband and wife in a relationship characterized by grace-filled headship and submission, it confronts the culture with the power of the gospel. When a single man or woman is chaste for the glory of God, it speaks with piercing clarity. When men or women—married or single—are distinctively masculine or feminine with other men and women in the workplace, they serve as a clarion call for people to be saved by Christ in order to live as God intended and nature urges.

To produce Christians with these bravely counter-cultural lives, pastors have to equip the saints for the work of ministry to one another *and* to a watching and desperate world. Christ was crucified as a *public* spectacle (Gal. 3:1).[21] Christians are to be salt and light in the *world* (Matt. 5:13-16). Christians are to *show the world* we are disciples by the way we love one another (John 13:35) in the household of God and in those distinct relationships (marriage being one) in that household (Eph. 5 and 6).

The Christian faith and life cannot, as we sometimes hear, be private because the gospel is not a private truth. Jesus claims the whole world in His death—in truth, He reclaims it for God, staking it as His own. From this Christological launchpoint, we display and declare the Gospel through transformed lives that reflect redeemed masculinity and femininity. In this way, we not only confront the culture with

---

21. See Owen Strachan, 'The Wilberforce Test: Preaching and the Public Square,' *9Marks*, November 11, 2014, accessible at http://9marks.org/article/the-wilberforce-test-preaching-and-the-public-square. For a deeper take on the role of pastors as public theologians, see Kevin Vanhoozer and Owen Strachan, *The Pastor as Publc Theologian: Reclaiming a Lost Vision* (Grand Rapids: Baker Academic, 2015).

the great truths of biblical sexuality—we live on mission as men and as women.

The battle is a mission moment

Of course, the mission of the church is to make disciples of all nations, by preaching the gospel, baptizing them and gathering them into churches to be taught (Matt. 28:18-20). But disciples must be equipped for mission by having a gospel-centered understanding of all things. We declare the whole counsel of God (Acts 20:27). Biblical sexuality affects all areas of life as we have seen. We enter the world for mission, not as politicians, but as cross-shaped theologians, able to recognize the bite points where the battle rages, bold to enter in to declare and display the truth of the gospel.

Pornography, adultery, homosexual marriage and trans-genderism are not the main issues. Sin is the issue which makes engaging the culture with biblical sexuality a gospel opportunity. It's a mission moment. At the very worst of times, when Satan seems to have the upper hand, God is using it for victory. Just look at the cross. For this battle we need Christians who are passionate but sober-minded, who think biblically and pray earnestly, and who will speak the truth in love.

The church must speak in the battle

The real issue is whether the church will be silent. The silence of Adam was at the heart of the fall. Adam didn't speak up in the Garden when Satan was attacking his wife and undermining God's truth. The church must not be silent for fear of imposition and offence. Yet many Christians are not emboldened because many pastors are not emboldened. They might sometimes speak on biblical sexuality and then only vaguely. They might teach complementarity but not thoroughly.

In such circumstances, the church can become, even without knowing it, functionally egalitarian. The egalitarian impulse has weakened its doctrine. God wants something better. He wants the church to be equipped to practically live out complementarity and theologically defend it in the public square. Pastors need to equip the saints for this (Eph. 4:11-12). Such work begins in the pulpit. So people must pray for, support and encourage their pastors in holding to this truth.

The Bible starts with a marriage in Genesis 2 and ends with one in Revelation 19. God made complementarian marriage good and it was always made to point to the good news: Christ and His saving love for the church (Eph. 5:32). That's what everyone needs because everyone is a sinner before God.

We don't want to destroy and discourage people; we want to win them. And we want to present a compelling gospel-shaped world to the culture through biblical manhood and womanhood. It's about God's authority to design His world. This is a mission moment that will define the church. It will test evangelicalism because where you stand on sexuality in the home, the church and the world will indicate your trust in the authority and sufficiency of the Bible. But it is also the battleground where souls can be won for Christ.

This battle for a world of love and order is raging. We take heart in remembering this: 'where the battle rages, the loyalty of the soldier is proved.' May God find us faithful on the day when Christ returns.

CHAPTER FIVE

What Does the Church Have to Say About Our Sexualized Age?

She was not the kind of young woman you would think was on her way to stardom. From a broken home, she bounced from school to school, known for a loud laugh and a certain toughness. In her youth, while everyone else was listening to Slipknot and Papa Roach, she chanced upon an Etta James record in a music shop and was soon transfixed. Not long after, this young woman from a troubled background signed a record deal. A few years later, her major-label album caught fire; a few years after that, in 2015, she was firmly established as one of the top artists in the world.

If you had seen Adele Laurie Blue Adkins in her younger days, you might have felt pity for her. You might have worried about her. But despite the trauma and trials of her early life, Adele found a way to channel her gifts into a career. She might have seemed normal. But inside Adele, there was tremendous power, tremendous musical ability, just waiting to burst out. Her background made her easy to underestimate. But her talent, nurtured over time, eventually made her hard to miss.

You read about Adele's incredible story and are reminded of the capacities of human beings. Within all of us there is God-given potential and ability. There is a cheesy way to celebrate this today—everyone getting a trophy just for showing up—but there is also a profoundly Christian way to do so. We locate ingenuity and artistry and achievement in the Creator's design. We are the image of God, and capable of great things.

There is more than just the capacity for creativity in us, however. We surprise ourselves not only by our inherent abilities, but also something less encouraging. Every person has an inherent capacity for anger and unrighteousness that sometimes stuns us. No one teaches us this; we don't go to school, most of us, to get a degree in 'Spontaneous Cutting Remarks.' We tutor ourselves in this subject and many others: 'Secretly Congratulating Yourself on Your Awesomeness,' 'Coveting Without a Hint of Conscience,' and 'Blaming God When Things Get Tough' being just a few of them.

The human heart, Jeremiah says, is 'desperately wicked' in its natural state (Jer. 17:9). Even after redemption strikes, converting us to love Christ, we still must wrestle against the evil force inside us (see Col. 3:1-11). This is tough stuff in the age of self-esteem, when any challenge to our feelings gets labeled as mean, and the mention of any subject we don't like 'triggers' us. The Bible pulls no punches with humankind, however. We are evil by nature. Sin bubbles up from within. None of us do good on our own (Rom. 3:10-18). We all go astray. This is not fundamentally a horizontal problem, however, meaning that we simply do harm to ourselves and others. Our sin is at its core rebellion against God manifesting in ten thousand ways our natural hatred of God and His will.

The Protestant Reformers of the sixteenth century had a term for this problem: we are depraved, and this owes to original sin.[1] Thanks to Adam's fall, we are not fundamentally good. Our instincts so often run in the wrong directions. The evil actions that so clearly display our innate sinfulness are urged along by evil desires (see James 1:14). Something has gone terribly wrong with humanity. This the church has always known, but not only about the surrounding world. We know this about ourselves. We are those who cannot trust ourselves, who cannot depend on our own strength, and who have seen by the sheer grace of God that we *need help*. We need to be ruined and remade by the grace of God.

Today, a secular culture sharply challenges this thinking. It tells us that our theology of sin is injurious and our perspective on mankind is harmful. It urges us not to fight and master our natural desires, but to embrace them. It goes further: it whispers in our ear for us to take these sinful appetites and make them our identity, part of the words we use to describe ourselves. We Christians find ourselves in a tough position today. We are not only those who hold specific convictions

---

1. See, for starters, Timothy George, *Theology of the Reformers* (Nashville: Broadman Press, 1988), 213-16. For a magisterial if dense read on original sin and its implications, see Jonathan Edwards, *The Great Christian Doctrine of Original Sin Defended*, ed. Clyde A. Holbrook, vol. 3 of The Works of Jonathan Edwards (New Haven: Yale University Press, 1970).

about our manhood, womanhood, and sexual ethics. We are those who stand in the way of cultural progress as well!

Nowhere is this divide seen more clearly than in the debate over transgender and homosexual identity. In what follows, we examine these views in brief and present a biblical response to them, one shaped by the gospel of Christ.

Transgender Identity

I can recall the first time I saw a cross-dressing individual. I was in a coffee shop doing some reading as many a seminary student will do. While waiting for my latte (I have never been too fussy with my drink preferences), I stood behind a man now dressing as a woman. This was an unusual occurrence for me. Growing up in Maine, one did not see much of this sort of behavior.

I remember feeling both disturbed and saddened by this person's self-expression. I suspect many Christians feel similarly when we encounter people who try to embrace the look and behavior of the opposite sex as their own. Society used to view this behavior in terms of 'dysphoria,' recognizing rightly that it is a condition owing to personal disturbance, not health. Children who felt like they were a girl in a boy's body, for example, would receive careful counseling that would aim at helping them own their natural manhood or womanhood. People who suffered abuse and neglect, medical professionals realized, seemed much more likely to experience these inclinations.[2]

---

2. For a sound traditional perspective on transgender identity, see Paul McHugh, 'Transgender Surgery Isn't the Solution,' *Wall Street Journal*, June 12, 2014, accessible at http://www.wsj.com/articles/paul-mchugh-transgender-surgery-isnt-the-solution-1402615120. McHugh is the former psychiatrist-in-chief for Johns Hopkins Hospital and a nationally renowned specialist.

What society used to consider a treatable condition it now regards as a positive identity. The rise of 'transgender' ideology has taken many aback, but this cultural shift shows no signs of slowing. American society in particular is undergoing wrenching changes as lawmakers trip over themselves to pass new regulations indicating positive reception of 'transgender' individuals. The major laboratory for this cultural recon-struction is, fittingly, the restroom. In California, Maine, Washington, and other states, children whose 'gender identity' does not match their sex may enter restrooms and changing facilities of the opposite sex in various public places. Similar accommodations are popping up all over America and beyond.[3]

We can only characterize the cultural move to whole-heartedly approve and even abet transgender identity as per-verse and tragic. Of course, various societies have allowed individuals experiencing this condition to live their life; it is not necessarily a crime to fall into personal sin and confusion. But we find ourselves in a very different moment, one in which we are expected to norm and approve of unbiblical identities.

At base, in increasing measure societally, boys want to be girls, and girls want to be boys. Boys and girls adopt the traits, appearance, and traditional behaviors of the opposite sex. They do all the same things, address one another in the same colloquial language, and observe precious few customs and manners that distinguish one sex from another. Society encourages this shift and punishes those who push back against it. Our children, shockingly, are the ones who must bear the brunt of this push to neutralize the sexes. Adults by their very

---

3. For a taste of the way the discussion is going in one small American town, see Emmanuella Grinberg, 'Bathroom access for transgender teen divides Missouri town,' CNN, September 5, 2015, accessible at http://www.cnn.com/2015/09/03/living/missouri-transgender-teen-feat.

station in life should protect children in all ways and at all costs. But adults are precisely the ones who are engineering school systems, for example, to accept transgender ideology, a move that sets little ones up for confusion, fear, and even harm.[4]

It is important to note that much of the impetus for this change comes from boys wanting to be girls. Data on transgender individuals is notoriously hard to pin down, but most studies indicate that for every one woman who 'transitions' to manhood, three men 'transition' to womanhood.[5] Certainly it is men who are making the headlines, whether this means former decathlete Bruce Jenner adopting the name 'Caitlyn,' or boys in Chicago wanting to change in the girls' locker-room. Men, it seems, are negotiating a feminist world with little traditional knowledge. Faced with the prospect of female dominance, many seem to be choosing to become women rather than compete with them (as a secular order encourages).

Transgender ideology has freshly arrived on the scene, but this issue is not new. It is in fact ancient. The Bible speaks directly to the instinct to take on a personal identity that does not correspond with one's sex. Deuteronomy 22:5 addresses such a move: 'A woman shall not wear a man's garment, nor shall a man put on a woman's cloak, for whoever does these things is an abomination to the Lord your God.' Some readers might think that this text, falling under the now-fulfilled

4. A sound reference guide for these issues is the book by Ryan Anderson, *Truth Overruled: The Future of Marriage and Religious Freedom* (Regnery, 2015). Anderson approaches these matters from a 'natural law' perspective.

5. See Femke Olyslager and Lynn Conway, 'On the Calculation of the Prevalence of Transsexualism,' accessible at http://ai.eecs.umich.edu/people/conway/TS/Prevalence/Reports/Prevalence%20of%20Transsexualism.pdf. We do not necessarily indicate by citing this study that the authors would agree with our perspective on this matter.

Old Covenant law, has virtually no import for us in the 21ˢᵗ century. Aren't there other prohibitions against mixed fabrics in clothing in the old covenant?

There are, but Deuteronomy 22:5 speaks to a bigger matter than mere fashion choices in the Ancient Near East. This verse indissolubly connects morality with biology. In other words, if you are a man, you are called by God to dress like a man. If you are a woman, you are called by God to dress like a woman. To fail to honor God in one's body is to blaspheme divine design. To put it differently: biology is destiny. Your body is not lying to you. Your anatomy is telling you who you are, and who God made you to be.[6]

The New Testament reinforces the teaching of Deuteronomy 22. 1 Corinthians 11:1-16 has befuddled some readers, but it reinforces the point just made. Women and men should grow their hair different lengths, according to the Apostle Paul. 'Long hair,' he teaches, 'is a disgrace' for men but the 'glory' of a woman (1 Cor. 11:14-15). The man and woman united in marriage must not look the same or blur their roles in marriage. The man was not created for the woman, but the woman for the man (1 Cor. 11:9). The thrust of this complex passage is the following:

1) Men and women are not the same, and should not present themselves physically as if this is so.
2) In taking care to honor distinctions between the sexes, we display the order of creation, with the man as the leader of his wife.

---

6. This is the argument made by Denny Burk in an important book chapter on these matters. See Burk, 'Training Our Kids in a Transgender World,' in Owen Strachan and Jonathan Parnell, eds., *Designed for Joy: How the Gospel Impacts Men and Women, Identity and Practice* (Wheaton, IL: Crossway, 2015), 89-98.

These are contested words in our time. But we note that Paul here reinforces the original plan of God for men and women.[7] His teaching is not new; it is ancient, connected to the original code of God's set-apart, covenantal people.

The Corinthian church found itself in a situation remarkably like ours. To help it, Paul drew the church's attention back to the goodness of God-made manhood and womanhood. The people of Corinth might experiment with gender fluidity, but the people of God could not. The people of Corinth might distance themselves from biblical roles, but the people of God had no such option. Christians are not *reflexively* masculine and feminine. We are *doxologically* masculine and feminine. We know that the way we dress and present ourselves and even think about ourselves renders glory to our Maker when biblically faithful.[8]

The preceding leads us to the following conclusion: transgender ideology is not only disordered. It is immoral. It is wrong. We must not cross-dress, blur the boundaries between the sexes, and downplay the creative intent of God. When God saves us, He does for us what He did for the Corinthians: He opens our eyes to the beauty of His handiwork. Too

---

7. Books marking the distinctions between men and women are not commonplace, but thankfully such resources do exist. See Wayne Grudem and Bruce A. Ware, *Biblical Foundations for Manhood and Womanhood* (Wheaton, IL: Crossway, 2002); Wayne Grudem and Dennis Rainey, *Pastoral Leadership for Manhood and Womanhood* (Wheaton, IL: Crossway, 2003).

8. Texts that helpfully flesh out the practices of womanhood include Mary A. Kassian, *Girls Gone Wise in a World Gone Wild* (Chicago, IL: Moody Publishers, 2010); Mary A. Kassian and Nancy DeMoss, *True Woman 101: A Divine Design: An Eight-Week Study on Biblical Womanhood* (Chicago, IL: Moody Publishers, 2012). On the practices of manhood, see Mark Chanski, *Manly Dominion: In a Passive-Purple-Four-Ball World* (Lincroft, NJ: Calvary Press, 2007); Randy Stinson and Dan Dumas, *A Guide to Biblical Manhood* (Louisville, KY: SBTS Press, 2011).

often, evangelicals savor the aesthetic wisdom of God seen in the mountains but ignore the master-stroke of God's work in humankind. At the height of His creative streak, He forms Adam from the dust of the ground. The woman He makes from the man, forever linking their destinies. Manhood and womanhood are gifts, He instructs us, not burdens. These realities are not incidental; they are fundamental.

This moral stance does not preclude compassionate counseling for people who feel like they are trapped in the wrong body. This kind of perspective flows from the first sin of Adam and Eve. In sinning against God, in allowing Satan to subvert the created order, Adam and Eve welcomed a host of sinful behaviors and identities into the world. One of these is the temptation to pull away from one's God-given sex. The modern way of presenting such a mindset is to separate 'gender identity' from bodily form. But we cannot separate the two. God Himself has not lied to us in giving us our body. This is the identity He has chosen for us. We do not have the freedom to remake ourselves. We have the freedom to receive His good gifts and, through Christ our Savior, treasure them.[9]

If a man or woman feels like they should cross-dress, we should compassionately engage this desire. This means, at base, asking good questions: Why do they feel this way? Is there trauma in their background? How do they understand personal identity? We will need to ask good questions, listen well, and respond to them in compassion as a fellow sinner. In our counseling, we should make clear that we too experience ungodly temptation. The answer for all such inclinations,

---

9. For more on the theology of the body with respect to these issues, see Albert Mohler, *We Cannot Be Silent: Speaking Truth to a Culture Redefining Sex, Marriage, and the Very Meaning of Right and Wrong* (Nashville, TN: Thomas Nelson, 2015).

however, is to understand and appropriate the moral clarity of God's will. It is loving to lead struggling sinners to apprehend the wisdom of God. This means, in practical terms, that we help those who experience gender dysphoria to know that, even as they work through their past and examine the root causes of their struggles, they will find happiness and glorify God only by obeying His Word.

Obeying God's Word on this question means confessing sinful inclinations, repenting of them, and forming godly habits in order to own one's God-given identity. The gospel does not exempt us from digging through our messy temptations. It summons us to confront them, and to do so over the course of months, years, and a lifetime. It is not sound to cross-dress as one works through transgender matters. If we feel pulled to such behaviors, we will need to repent, and to turn away from acting on them.

It may well be that the Spirit's sanctifying work in us over time causes these desires to lessen. If they remain to some degree, however, we must reckon with them the same way we would with any sinful bent: we should pray to master them, fight them in the moment by focusing on Christ, and repent if we stray from God's will. This may be a new issue at the mass-culture level, but gender dysphoria is as old as the fall. There is no separate gospel for people who experience it. Alongside discerning counseling from wise elders, the solution to this proclivity is found in God.

We must not think that the rise of transgender ideology has no relevance for the vast majority of evangelicals. It surely does. If nothing else, this trend has opened the church's eyes to see that we must take complementarity seriously. Our past devaluation of manhood and womanhood has not served us well in our quest to help those who suffer sexually. The gender-neutralization of the culture and to some degree the church has left us without eyes to see the aesthetic wisdom of God in our form and role. If we have embraced a blurred Christianity that downplays divine design, we will not be well-positioned to offer gospel answers to our culture and gospel counsel to our neighbors.

This is an ironic discovery. Just when evangelicals thought they had scrubbed their faith of any serious tie to gender, and thus had distanced themselves from the more embarrassing parts of biblical sexual ethics, the culture decided to launch a gender revolution. Now, people who have for years downplayed manhood and womanhood find themselves in an awkward place: they may either side with the culture and lose meaningful comprehension of the sexes, or they may side with the Scripture and swallow what they have previously pushed off their plate. I suppose we could say it like this: we are all complementarians now, at least when it comes to personal identity.

Some evangelicals may have worked strenuously to avoid the 'gender wars,' but anyone who does not agree with the cultural revolution unfolding around us must know that such avoidance is no longer an option. Whether we want to face this matter or not, it has arrived on our doorstep. At both the societal and the personal level, we must have an answer to share, and a gospel word to offer. Thankfully, in all these things, the Scripture is sufficient—but not only sufficient. It is living and active, alive to the challenges we face, poised to pour delicious clarity into wells drained of truth.

Homosexuality

The major issue of our time is homosexuality. The church has not asked for this. We do not address this matter as an obsession for us. Many of us find ourselves speaking much more about it than we want to. Homosexuality is not the cardinal sin for evangelicals. We are not preoccupied with it. But God desires that we would speak the whole counsel of His will, and so like the prophets and apostles we cannot help but address the major issues of our time. We speak up because we know that if we do not do so we fail to honor God and promote the truth that claims every inch of creation.

The modern view of homosexuality as a positive state owes to a widespread acceptance of sexuality as an orientation. Here is how the American Psychological Association (APA) has defined sexual orientation:

> Sexual orientation refers to an enduring pattern of emotional, romantic, and/or sexual attractions to men, women, or both sexes. Sexual orientation also refers to a person's sense of identity based on those attractions, related behaviors, and membership in a community of others who share those attractions.[10]

In this conception, sexual orientation is a state of being. Same-sex attraction is a constituent part of one's identity. While we will reject this view, we do note that the APA connects an 'enduring pattern' of sexual attraction to orientation. You desire something over and over and the APA considers you to be 'oriented' toward that end. This is a workable definition for our purposes.

Though it is now constantly a subject of cultural discussion, homosexuality is no new struggle. It is, like the desire to cross-dress, an ancient inclination. The Scripture is not outmoded on this or any other matter. In both the Old and New Testaments, it presents unmistakably clear guidance on the prospect of

---

10. American Psychological Association, 'Answers to Your Questions: For a Better Understanding of Sexual Orientation and Homosexuality,' accessible at http://www.apa.org/topics/lgbt/orientation.pdf.

members of the same sex engaging in sexual behavior. The Bible addresses homosexuality in exclusively negative terms (see Genesis 19; Leviticus 18:22; Deuteronomy 23:17-18; Romans 1:26-27; 1 Corinthians 6:9; 1 Timothy 1:10).[11] We will consider the teaching of two of these crucial texts. First, we look at the witness of Leviticus 18:22, which handles homosexuality as part of a group of evil practices:

> You shall not give any of your children to offer them to Molech, and so profane the name of your God: I am the LORD. You shall not lie with a male as with a woman; it is an abomination. And you shall not lie with any animal and so make yourself unclean with it, neither shall any woman give herself to an animal to lie with it: it is perversion (Lev. 18:21-23).

It is important to situate the old covenant witness on homosexuality within God's broader sexual ethic. If we remember the core material from Chapter One on complementarity, then we will know that the will of God for sexual expression is marital intimacy. There is no other moral, God-approved, God-honoring context for sexual activity.[12] The passage above indicates that homosexuality fits within a pagan ethic, one that includes a total rejection of divine design: killing one's children as opposed to caring for them, having sex with a member of the same sex as opposed to one's spouse, and pursuing sex with an animal as opposed to ruling over the beasts per the teaching of Genesis 1.

We thus must not isolate homosexuality. It is a part of paganism, a God-denying worldview that views the body as

---

11. For a richly biblical take on this subject, see Kevin DeYoung, *What Does the Bible Really Teach about Homosexuality?* (Wheaton, IL: Crossway, 2015).

12. For more on this biblical truth, see Denny Burk, *What is the Meaning of Sex?* (Wheaton, IL: Crossway, 2013).

a vehicle for the fulfillment of one's inherent sexual desires.[13] The pagan mind does not honor distinctions between the sexes, nor roles between the sexes. Paganism divinizes the creation and, in doing so, collapses all God-made boundaries. From this standpoint, it encourages people to indulge their sexual appetites, whatever they may be.

This is no new mindset. It is as ancient as the serpent's hiss. Paganism is the mirror worldview to the biblical one. Where God creates distinct sexes, paganism blurs them. Where God creates distinct roles, paganism denies them. Where God elevates man to a position of stewardship of the creation, paganism dethrones him and encourages him to act like a beast. The instinct to pursue our base sexual desires, to unleash our sexual appetites, owes not to the sexual revolution of the 1960s, but to the fall of mankind thousands of years ago.

Homosexuality represents the pagan response to God's plan for marriage. Marriage, as we saw in Chapter Four, is created as a complementarian institution. God designed it not simply to display the beauty of earthly complementarity between one man and one woman, but to dazzle the cosmos through the covenantal union of Christ the Savior and the church His redeemed possession. Earthly marriage, then, is not its own end. It has always pointed to something much, much greater.

This is a huge part of why Christians advocate for marriage in the public square. We recognize human flourishing as a major concern of ours. But while we make the best possible arguments from reason and design that we can, our stake in marriage is impossibly higher than our short lifespan allows. Our stake in marriage is cosmic. It is covenantal. Marriage

---

13. Peter Jones has contributed eye-opening work on the matter of paganism. See Jones, *Pagans in the Pews: Protecting Your Family and Community from the Pervasive Influence of the New Spirituality* (Ventura, CA: Regal, 2004).

tells the greatest truth there is: that God has faithfully kept His covenant to make a people for Himself, a people washed in the blood of the lamb.

All this homosexuality denies. Those inclined to this behavior, of course, may not know the full ramifications of their desires. They may not even fully understand the passions they possess and the instincts they feel. This is very often true of us as sinners. Our hearts course with darkness, frankly, and we rarely consciously choose ahead of time to indulge in sin. Evil bubbles up from within us. At times, of course, we do consciously set out to commit unrighteousness. But oftentimes, sin erupts from our heart, unbidden and undetected until the moment of detonation.

This is true of ten thousand different perversities we carry within us. We explode at a friend because of jealousy that festers. They have what we want, and so we cut them down to size. We gorge ourselves on sexual images, taking what is not ours while feeling it is owed to us. We ignore our loved ones, focusing on our own pursuits, absent from their lives. In more ways than we could count, we give vent to our sins, in many cases from desires that surge in our bloodstreams without warning. Sin is not a little knife that we take out on occasion to do a little damage. Sin is a raging fire, consuming whole forests by a spark, that if not battled and mastered by the Spirit will consume us.[14]

---

14. For more on how lustful desires are sinful, see Owen Strachan, 'A Referendum on Depravity: Same-Sex Attraction as Sinful Desire,' *Journal for Biblical Manhood & Womanhood* XX.1 (Spring 2015), 24-34. You can access this article free on the CBMW website at http://cbmw.org/wp-content/uploads/2015/04/4.1_Referendum-Depravity_Owen-Strachan.pdf. Key to this argument is the reality expressed in James 1, namely, that our own sinful desires 'lure and entice' us to commit wickedness. See also Denny Burk and Heath Lambert, *Transforming Homosexuality: What the Bible Says about Sexual Orientation and Change* (Phillipsburg, NJ: P&R Publishing, 2015).

Every sin, every little white lie, separates us by an infinite distance from God. We cannot miss this. But this historic Christian affirmation cannot obscure the fact that some sins do involve a deeper denial of God's wisdom and plan than others. This is the culmination of Paul's argument in Romans 1:22-27. Here, he links the creation order with the evil nature of homosexuality:

> Claiming to be wise, they became fools, and ex-changed the glory of the immortal God for images resembling mortal man and birds and animals and creeping things. Therefore God gave them up in the lusts of their hearts to impurity, to the dishonoring of their bodies among themselves, because they ex-changed the truth about God for a lie and worshiped and served the creature rather than the Creator, who is blessed forever! Amen.
>
> For this reason God gave them up to dishonorable passions. For their women exchanged natural rela-tions for those that are contrary to nature; and the men likewise gave up natural relations with women and were consumed with passion for one another, men committing shameless acts with men and re-ceiving in themselves the due penalty for their error (Rom. 1:22-27).

The evangelical inclination to separate divine design from sexuality simply will not work in this passage. Paul traces the stirrings of homosexuality to the subversion of the created order. In other words, we must not think that homosexual desire is problematic merely because it's not what God intended in terms of sexual expression. Homosexuality proceeds from what we have called paganism according to the apostolic mind. The line of thought here is this:

> First, man exalts himself over God, thinking himself 'wise' (22).
>
> Second, he worships the creation through 'images' (23).
>
> Third, God gives people up to the 'lusts of their hearts,' which are impure (24).
>
> Fourth, this means, as verses 25-27 make clear, that sinners like us become 'consumed with passion' of a homosexual kind and thus give up 'natural relations' for homosexual behavior.
>
> Fifth, in verse 32, we learn that indulging these appetites leads not simply to more indulgence, but to advocacy of the same.

This passage in Romans 1 shows us that we cannot see homosexuality as an isolated sin. It is connected to a broader web of deception. There is a perverse logic to it. If we deny God's rulership, then we worship this earth. If we worship the earth, then we do not fight our sinful lusts and passions, but view them as virtuous. If we view them as virtuous, we do what comes naturally: we engage in the behaviors that our desires crave. The final step makes sense as well: we don't confine our thirst for this sexual sin to our own private lives, but advocate for it and approve of it.

We cannot miss the prescience of Paul's thought. Writing in the first century, he has described the twenty-first century with stunning precision. We Christians find ourselves midstream in terms of the culture. The tide is pulling against us. We are not supposed to go in the direction of God. The energy of our society seeks to draw us away and compromise our convictions. All around us, people not only practice sinful lifestyles, but advocate for them. Paul was right. He wrote to the people of Corinth, a city awash in sexual sin. He sought to help them understand the radical nature of their context. His strong and strikingly direct words help us, too. They make sense of our cultural moment. We find ourselves in a new sexual revolution, and we are here in this rushing stream because many around us practice the five-fold outline above.

Next Steps for Christians Today

We will all face the brave new sexual order discussed in this brief chapter for the rest of our lives. While much further study is needed here, we can target three key responses for the church in such a climate.

First, we need to speak the truth, and the whole truth, about homosexuality. Many of us seek some kind of third way to address homosexuality. We feel weird having such a stubbornly moral perspective. But our charge as believers is to declare the mind of God and watch as the Holy Spirit convicts, converts, and conforms. There is no place in the Bible that requires us to soften the declared will of God. Nothing in Scripture needs reworking. Nothing is insufficient. Nothing is deficient. The Word of God is pure as mountain snow. Our charge is to tell the truth about all sin, and point our hearers to Christ as the remedy.

Second, we need to help sinners like us find their way. The church must simultaneously declare the truth and minister it. We must hold out the hope of life change and personal transformation. Our sin is crucified with Christ (Rom. 6:6). If we are in Christ, we have died to sin. We have a new nature, a new name, and a new hope. For people struggling with sexual sin, including homosexuality, this may not mean that conversion equals instant eradication of temptation. The battle against sinful desires may take a lifetime to unfold. If so, God will gain much glory through our fight, which is propelled by recognizing that same-sex attraction requires repentance. We have no ability in biblical terms to approve of 'gay Christianity' or any kind of Christianity married to a pattern of sin.[15]

This is true whether we watch an extended scene or entertain fallen thoughts for just a moment or two. The Scripture calls us to repent of our lusts (Matt. 5:21-30). In Romans 1, Paul does not only indict sinful behavior, but lusts and passions contrary to God's will. In any moment when we feel a pull to something evil, whether coveting a luxury good, a vengeful outcome, a gluttonous thirst, a perverse sexuality, a harmful interest in children, or personal exaltation, we must confess our sin and repent. We do not confess and repent only for sinful inclinations we entertain for a minute or longer. There is no such biblical stipulation. We have hearts of darkness. When we hunger after things that are inherently evil, we should in any and all cases confess such hunger to God and immediately repent in the name and power of Jesus Christ.

We want a zero-tolerance approach to sin—all sin. We do not wish to manage our sin like accounts in a bank. We have no peace with sin. We want to hunt it down, put a hood over its head, and kill it. We hate sin. It is our enemy. We know that if we do not go on the offensive against it, it will surely go on the offensive against us. So we confess not only our sinful deeds, but our sinful thoughts and inclinations. God wants us

---

15. See R. Albert Mohler, Jr., ed., *God and the Gay Christian? A Response to Matthew Vines* (Louisville: SBTS Press, 2014).

139

to repent not simply of the big sins, but the little ones as well. This is true of lust after people of the opposite sex who are not our spouse; this is true of same-sex attraction.

Such practice is not over-scrupulous. It is not defeatist. It will not breed despair. What will breed despair is the failure to turn from one's sinful inclinations and behaviors. To fall into that pattern means that we no longer take our sin seriously. Doing so places us in grave danger. Those of us who desire to glorify God with every fiber of our existence will do well to see that repentance is not the ground of sorrow, but of freedom. Confessing our sinful desires, even the secret and fleeting ones, opens up the gateway to joy. All around us are people who live in entrapment. They never confess their sins to God, they never repent, and their hearts are open wounds. We must not think that they have it good, and we who are called to repent have it bad. Repentance is the gateway to delight, for it leads us to God who is true delight itself.

When someone comes to us and confesses a bent toward homosexuality, we do not castigate them as if they are perverse and we are not. We acknowledge that we carry sin within us just as they do. We talk through their past, their present, and help them see that their history is not their destiny. Through Christ, they have power over sin. We do not know what God has for them. He may lead them to marry, or He may call them to lifelong celibacy. Either way, His call to holiness is not a weight around the neck. The call to holiness is a summons to happiness. We do not, after all, stumble our way across the narrow path, lurching and alone. When God leads us to this path, we walk beside Christ, and we find a body of believers all around us. Our local church helps bear our burdens and share our sorrows. It enters into our joy and unites with us as a family, the true family which will live together throughout all eternity and beyond.[16]

The world thinks it offers us liberation by advocating for sexual license. But this is a lie. It is Christ who offers us liberation. It is Christ who frees us from the power of sin. It is Christ who intercedes for us as we wage war on the flesh. It is Christ who strengthens us through the Spirit when we feel weak and lonely and defeated. The hope of the Christian who experiences same-sex attraction is the same hope of every Christian: Christ in us, and Christ coming back for us. There is no separate spirituality and no separate gospel for Christians who experience temptations of various kinds. There is one Lord and one baptism.

Third, we need to develop a broader sexual ethic. The church must tell the truth. It must extend grace to needy sinners. But it must also play the long game and develop in the local assembly a bigger, richer understanding of complementarity and sexuality. We cannot simply handle the most pressing issues and assume all is well. We need to build out a robust sexual ethic, one grounded in complementarity, alive to the beauty of manhood and womanhood, enthralled with marriage, and focused on comprehensive personal holiness as the very channel of God's glory in our lives.[17] Now is not the time for local churches to play small ball, in other words, to quieten the Scripture's witness on these

---

16. Two powerful testimonies of triumph over a homosexual lifestyle are Rosaria Champagne Butterfield, *Secret Thoughts of an Unlikely Convert* (Pittsburgh, PA: Crown & Covenant Publications, 2013); Sam Allberry, *Is God Anti-Gay? and Other Questions about Homosexuality, the Bible and Same-Sex Attraction* (Epsom, Surrey: Good Book, 2015).

17. For help in fashioning a convictional and gracious public witness, see Russell Moore, *Onward: Engaging the Culture without Losing the Gospel* (Nashville, TN: B&H Books, 2015).

matters. Now is the time to help people that the stakes are impossibly high.

As part of this work, we must encourage men to be men and women to be women. We've already spelled out a good deal of what this entails biblically in previous chapters. For now, though, we want to be clear that it is good for men and women to dress in distinct ways. It is good for men to look like men, to talk like men, and to act like men. It is good for women to look like women, to talk like women, and to act like women. No person is the living archetype of masculinity and femininity, of course. Further, we don't want to buy into exaggerated sexual differences. But we do need to remember that Paul himself calls for men and women to present themselves in distinct and differentiated ways.

We want our boys to pursue strength, to look adults in the eye when they talk, to shake hands with a firm grip, to welcome physical challenges, to take responsibility in the home, to wear clothes that are not feminine, to play games that are masculine, to jump to their feet when a woman needs assistance and offer it discreetly and courageously, and to appropriately and within reason pursue personal appearance and behavior that is not feminine. We do not want boys to talk to girls like they are are 'bros,' to embrace other boys as if they are their wives, to be snarky and passive-aggressive in their humor, and to shirk from responsibility and leadership.

We want our girls to pursue femininity, to develop a sense of social grace and decorum, to avoid being catty or enticing in their demeanor, to welcome opportunities to develop domestic skills, to wear clothes that are not masculine but are modestly feminine, to welcome physical exertion but avoid manly competition, and to appropriately and within reason pursue personal appearance and behavior that is not masculine. We do not want girls to treat boys like they are 'girlfriends,' to look to boys for meaning and self-worth, to be aggressive in their approach, and to shirk from a uniquely feminine manner.

We have all been influenced by an instinct that flows out of the fall. In Chapter Four, we called it an 'egalitarian impulse.' It's in all of us, and just like our wicked father the devil, it encourages us to blur all boundaries, deny the beauty of the sexes, and profane the Author of our humanity. We need to take care that we resist and overcome the egalitarian impulse. Manhood and womanhood do look slightly different in diverse cultures. There are surely gray areas in life that we must approach with wisdom and discernment. We do not want to jump beyond Scripture in our zeal for holiness.

But God loves masculinity and femininity. He made each. It is His desire that we, as much as we can, discern how to most clearly and doxologically live as God-made men and God-made women. Doing so in our time will glorify God and offer evangelistic witness to a world that desperately needs it. Who knew that something as small as your choice of outerwear could help to show people that God is real, and that Jesus redeems us as men and as women?

Conclusion

We all have tremendous natural potential. Like the famous singer Adele, we can put this potential to work in ways that display the uniqueness of God's image-bearing creation. Mankind is pre-loaded with dignity and worth and ability. But this is the bad news alongside the good news: we also have tremendous potential for evil in our hearts. We are born sinful. From the cradle to the grave, sin comes naturally. We are thus faced with a choice: will we obey the flesh or God in our earthly existence?

When we honor divine design, we send up a cheer in heaven. When we give into sexual temptation, we obey the serpent and gratify our pagan instincts. This is true, however, not simply of people who experience same-sex attraction. It is true of all of us. None of us is exempt from the fleshly hunger for *porneia*, or what our English translations call 'sexual immorality.' We all want what is not ours to have. We all are drawn to sexual expression outside of the covenant of marriage. On this matter, we all have sin to confess. We all leave the safety of the city of God to explore the wildness of the badlands. We do this in our thoughts, on our iPads, in our work flirtations, and a thousand other settings for sin.

For people like us, the holiness of God must loom large. We need something more than just tips and practices to help us set aside sinful entanglements. We need a fresh vision of God before our eyes. God is the one who will power us through our days and overcome our temptations. Savoring His presence and His design will remind us that there is a bigger story at work here than behavior management. Our part in the story is this: to freshly deny the serpent of lies his victory, day after day, and choose Christ, over and over again, as redeemed men and redeemed women.

CHAPTER SIX

Is Complementarity a 'Take it or Leave it' Doctrine?

I don't know if you've ever had your appendix out. If the answer is no, then take a moment and pray a prayer of thanksgiving. If the answer is yes, then you may—like me—have experienced some of the purest pain this world affords. I was ten when my appendix suddenly activated and decided to begin assaulting my body with waves of pain. To this day, twenty-four years later, I have no idea why it awakened. I ate a sugarless brownie at snacktime at school, and have since laid the blame at the feet of the sugarless brownie, slayer of boys everywhere.

Though I came within a few hours of it bursting, I survived the showdown with my roguish appendix. I was recently reflecting on that strange episode and realized that evangelicals treat certain areas of theology like the appendix. We sometimes hear that the gospel is super-important and that most else is take-it-or-leave-it. The structure of the local church? Not really important. Eschatological view? Not a pressing matter. The sovereignty of God in salvation? Too tough of an issue to think much about.

With a tough issue that folks disagree on, we often ignore it. We live and let live. But when the appendix flares, we freak out, and realize we've got to do something about it. This can be true with complementarity. But as we have seen, complementarity is vital to Christian identity and to personal flourishing. In what follows, we consider seven areas of life—important areas—that relate to complementarity. This chapter thus functions as an opportunity to pull together preceding insights and unfold them as one unified vision, showing that complementarity cannot be 'take it or leave it.' This is both a summary and a synthesis, then.

The vision given us of our manhood and womanhood allows us to see with unclouded eyes how complementarity is vital to our spiritual health. Christian manhood and womanhood are, in the end, nothing other than the outworking of a heart seized by the gospel and a mind bent on personal transformation.

Now, to our seven points.

First, complementarity shows us that humanity is brimming with purpose. God decided, in His infinite wisdom, to create not one sex, but two. Just as He made multiform diversity in the creation, forming the antelope and the Andes, the salamander and the Sierras, so He made one race of humanity in two sexes. The Lord loves diversity. He loves harmony. He desires that we sing one glorious song of praise to Him, but with different parts. He Himself fits this mold as a Trinitarian God.

God gave certain roles to the man and the woman. He did not desire that they do exactly the same thing. He made the man strong to work; He made the woman able to nurture life. There is tremendous potential spring-loaded into our manhood and womanhood. God does not call all of us to the same degree of realization of this potential. But that does not obscure the fact that the Lord has filled us with immense purpose as men and women. We should not look at our God-given bodies and think, 'Is this all there is? How boring!' We should marvel at what God enables us to do through the gift of a manly body or a womanly body.

The world would tell us that only some of us have potential. The world loves to pick winners and losers. It delights in grinding people down. The fallenness of creation means that there is a downward pull in this life. We read a news story about the dissolution of a celebrity's life and we snicker. We take joy in gossiping about the misfortunes of others. Since we often feel like a failure, we are tempted to pull others down with us, and so we feel conflicted about those who have great potential, and who struggle through tremendous odds to become successful. Sometimes we applaud them; too often, we tear them down.

This is not the way God designed things. God built incredible capacities into men and women. He filled us with promise when He made our first father and mother. He charged the man to lead in taking dominion of all things, a call that entailed steady work, creativity, stewardship, entrepreneurship, an aesthetic impulse, and so much more. He gave the woman the truly unbelievable chance to bear a living child in her body and then to nurture the child once born. These are not rote duties. They are propulsive capacities. God has invested every human being, man or woman, with more dignity, worth, and potential than we will ever know or appreciate.

Complementarity alone recognizes these unique abilities. Unlike Western societies that slouch their way to gender-neutralization, the church of God celebrates the uniqueness of manhood and womanhood. The Lord has not made us TeleTubbies, androgynous creatures that look and feel the same (the only indicator of difference being obnoxious pastel colors). He has made us men or women. The Lord wants us to seize our inborn potential as a man or woman and glorify Him in our body. Manhood and womanhood proceed from the very mind and design of Almighty God. Each is the very gift of God, not an accident of biology.

Second, complementarity helps us understand our sinful instincts. We are all alike in that we were born sinners. There's no special class of person who is born worse than another evildoer. In Adam, we are all lost. We are all depraved. We are all deserving of eternal damnation in hell. We manifest this sinful nature in numerous ways, with men and women overlapping in many practices, behaviors, and thought-patterns.

But we cannot flatten manhood and womanhood on this subject. There are certain temptations that one sex generally experiences more than the other. Adam abandoned his wife in the garden. He heard the Lord curse him and tell him, essentially, that he would be cruelly domineering over his wife and family. Eve led her husband into sin and then was cursed to seek out this sinful pattern. She would now struggle to trust him and submit to him. In these and other struggles, the sexes would wage war against one another and, ultimately, against God Himself.

Biblical complementarity opens our eyes to see that our sin sometimes, and in crucial ways, takes on sex-specific forms. Men are sorely tempted to take advantage of women. We do not want to receive God's call to maturity as Adam did. We want to delay growing up, to gratify our natural instincts, and just have fun. For those of us called to marriage, we don't want to wash our wives with the water of the Word (Eph. 5). We want to pursue our own interests. We don't listen well, and we get gruff with our wives just when they are opening up to us (contra 1 Pet. 3:7). These are not the only sins we commit; sometimes we're tempted to be domineering and sometimes we struggle not to be effeminate. Different men have different battles. But the Bible itself calls our attention to certain sins that are common to men.

So too with women. Women are tempted to usurp God-constituted authority, to grasp for leadership in certain spheres that the Lord has allotted, in His infinite wisdom, to men. This can be true even for women who say they love the Bible. Though they may be formally complementarian, they might undermine the leadership of men. This can surely happen in the home, according to 1 Peter 3:1-6. As Peter makes clear, it is all too easy to be formally committed to follow one's husband but informally frustrated with him. Different women have different battles, of course. Some women are too weak and not assertive enough in their marriages. But the Bible calls us to identify and overcome certain sins that are common to women.

Sin, we must always remember, is a multi-sided reality. It is not outside of us; even after we have been regenerated by the Holy Spirit through faith in Christ, sin bubbles up from within us. We cannot thus explain it away by blaming our circumstances as the cause of our sin. We sin from a heart that is new but not perfected. Men and women will sin in overlapping ways, being proud, quick to speak, slow to listen, and most significantly, by not loving God enough. But even as we share struggles, we must also see from Scripture that there are certain temptations common to men and women. We will be much less equipped to put our sin to death if we blind ourselves to this truth.

Third, complementarity provides us with a script for our lives. Our gender-neutral world wants to pretend that we are all the same, and that our plan for the future knows no variation. It is surely true that men and women are sometimes called to labor in shared enterprises. Many young men and women go to college; many men and women do full-time work, whether for all their lives or for a season; all Christians are called to pursue Christ personally, join a church, and help to advance the Great Commission however we can.

But the Bible offers us more than a one-size-fits-all faith. There are numerous realities that apply specifically to men and women, and that thus bring refreshing clarity to us. Wives, for example, know that they are uniquely called to have a 'gentle and quiet spirit,' a spirit that takes special expression in a marriage (1 Pet. 3:4). This teaching certainly applies most directly to married women, but we cannot miss the fact that any woman training her daughter in a godly way—knowing that marriage could be in her future—would teach her to develop by the Spirit's power such a posture. We cannot think that it is only when a woman gets married that she seeks to exhibit such godliness. It is far more reasonable to imagine that young women seeking to honor their Lord would read 1 Peter 3 and pray earnestly to the Lord to create in them such a counter-cultural spirit.

The Bible's script for wives, and for women who are training to emulate godly wives, is clear. A Christian woman conducts herself in a very different way than a woman trained in feminist views. Women of Christ, as we have spelled out earlier, welcome male leadership. Wherever possible, they support men of God as they seek to lead, even when men have not accrued vast amounts of experience in this role. Women pursue this kind of character well before they are actually married. They do so both to prepare for marriage and because the attitude Peter describes is a uniquely womanly attitude.

God intends for women to put their gifts and abilities to work for His glory. In this sense we see that Scripture, not the secular culture, offers women a truly revolutionary way of life. Wherever true complementarity has taken root, it has defied worldly notions of womanhood. This was true in the Greco-Roman world, so vaunted for its technological advances and sophisticated legal code. This context left women with vastly fewer rights and social agency than men. Husbands, for example, could and did conduct affairs with impunity, whereas women caught by their husbands in adultery could be killed without fear of legal action. To read such material is to recoil at the cruelty and wickedness of the world's conception of women.[1]

In contrast to the shackled woman of this era, the Bible presents a picture of a woman of agency. The Proverbs 31 woman, for example, owns her God-given role and in doing so leads a rich and full life. She makes wise decisions for her household, uses numerous skills in her daily work, conducts relationships with a wide variety of people in her community, and generally lives all-out for the glory of the Lord (Prov. 31:10-31). So it is in the New Testament. We

---

1. A helpful reference here is Bruce Winter, *Roman Wives, Roman Widows: The Appearance of New Women and the Pauline Communities* (Grand Rapids: Eerdmans, 2003).

glimpse women supporting the apostles through financial means, witnessing the empty tomb, serving in hospitality, helping disciple young believers, and much more.[2]

Here is a short selection of godly women in the NT, and their chief works.

- Joanna, 'the wife of Herod's steward Chuza,' likely contributed generous sums to Christ and His band of disciples (Luke 8:3).

- Priscilla helped her husband Aquila disciple Apollos, a learned and eloquent preacher (Acts 18:26).

- Timothy had both a godly mother and grandmother who trained him in the faith (2 Tim. 3:15).

- Tabitha was 'full of good works and acts of charity' (Acts 9:36).

- In a climate hostile to Christianity and thus dependent on home fellowships, Lydia and Mary each hosted gatherings of Christians (Acts 12:12; 16:13-15, 40).

- Phoebe was a 'servant of the church at Cenchrae,' a 'patron of many and of myself as well,' Paul noted in his letter to the Romans (Rom. 16:1-2).

- Junia (Rom. 16:7) and Apphia (Philem. 2) seem to have partnered with their husbands in gospel

---

2. For more on the distinct practices of godly women in the New Testament, see Owen Strachan, 'The Genesis of Gender and Ecclesial Womanhood,' *9Marks*, July 1, 2010, accessible at http://9marks.org/article/genesis-gender-and-ecclesial-womanhood. See also Courtney Reissig, *The Accidental Feminist: Restoring Our Delight in God's Good Design* (Wheaton, IL: Crossway, 2015).

ministry, whether through evangelism in the case of Junia or hosting a church in the case of Apphia.

• In the examples of Mary, Anna and others, we find women of persistent, reverential, bold, effectual prayer (Luke 1:46-55; 2:36-38).

This is a mere sampling of godly womanhood in Scripture. Clearly, the Bible gives women the green light to use their gifts and abilities in appropriate ways for the greater glory of God. It's not hard to find a role to play in God's kingdom for Christ-loving women—it can and should be easy.

Men too are given a script for their lives by Scripture. Most men are called to marriage, and that means that men must own the responsibility to transition from boyhood to manhood. The plan of God for most men is to leave their father and mother and win a woman's heart (Gen. 2:24). This is no small task, and it cannot and should not be done with a casual, shoulder-shrugging attitude. All boys should be trained to home in on the character of an elder as the mark of masculine maturity (1 Tim. 3:1-7; Titus 1:5-9).

We want our boys to look up to elders, not celebrities. We want to present them to Christ as those who love the Lord and serve Him with every fiber of their God-given strength. Pursuing the character of an elder involves careful preparation to be a husband and father (if God wills), and this means, in turn, committing oneself to holistic growth. Young men must reject the cultural call to immaturity in favor of the biblical call to maturity. Men need to spiritually lead themselves before they lead a wife and children. They need to go hard after a vocation that will provide for others in service of God's kingdom. They need to physically prepare their bodies to withstand challenges and protect those around them.

True manhood is not about benching huge amounts of weight, killing monsters in fantasy worlds, or drawing female attention. It's about drawing near to God. It's about the continual battle to forge disciplined habits so that you can kill sin and run without an anvil of guilt on your back. It's treating women well, seeing them as sisters, and thus approaching them 'with absolute purity' (1 Tim. 5:2). It's about learning to budget, groom yourself, look others in the eye when you're talking with them, hold the door for women, defend the weak, voluntarily inconvenience yourself so that others can stay dry and warm, pray, read the Bible, and serve the body of Christ. These are the practices of elders in your church. Make these the attributes you hunger and thirst for, not the attitudes and postures of oversized superheroes.

The Bible calls men to become something greater than they naturally are tempted to be. The Scripture calls men to forge character that welcomes self-sacrifice for the betterment of others, especially a wife. The gospel makes men who hate selfishness and crave selflessness. Every man should consider himself in training to be an elder or deacon. No man should be content with the culture's low expectations for him. He is not an animal, a goofball, or an idiot. God gives nobility to men, and asks that they make good on His gift. If a man has had little training in godly masculinity, he can know that the wind is at his back, and that the Lord wants him to start developing the character of a godly man immediately. This is the script for our lives that we need.

Fourth, complementarity tells us what our marriages most need. It is right and true that men and women are different. Our differences are no threat to us, as we have made clear. They are fashioned for our good and God's glory. Because we are not the same, husbands and wives must work hard to learn about one another, and to avoid seeing their spouse in abstract terms. We marry a specific person who has specific interests and desires and even needs.

But we must be careful not to push this thinking too far, or elevate it to a place of utmost importance. The single greatest key to marital happiness and flourishing is to follow the pattern of roles outlined in Ephesians 5:22-33. You may not know a ton about Mars, Venus, and love languages, but if you comprehend the dynamics of marriage (as outlined in chapter four), you are well on your way to developing a strong union. This is the key to a godly marriage—this, and not date nights, love languages, getaways, or any number of helpful practices.

The most important component of a healthy marriage is to know the theology of marriage, and thus to know what role one is to play in a theological marriage. Men are called to be Christlike heads who sacrifice themselves for the good of their wife, and women are called to be churchlike followers who submit to their husbands. Without this framework, marriages cannot give God the praise and honor He desires and deserves. Without this paradigm, men will not treat women as God intends, giving honor to them as the weaker vessel. Women, likewise, will not follow men as God intends, building them up as their Christlike head.

All sorts of techniques and tips can improve our marriages. Laying ground rules of communication, for example, will help both spouses. Doing activities that both husband and wife enjoy will foster togetherness and intimacy. Practical wisdom on sex cannot help but aid a young couple to navigate the new world of marital pleasure. We welcome advice and help in these areas, and every couple does well to seek out such assistance from older couples. But the key that unlocks a healthy marriage is known by Christians alone: that marriage is not made for its own sake, but for a God who has designed the earth's oldest institution to image the covenantal love of Christlike husband and churchlike wife.

Fifth, complementarity drives us to invest in the church's future. We cannot assume that men without shepherding will magically mature into elders. The church has a mandate to train men to be godly, and thus to lead the congregation. Too many churches are complementarian on paper but egalitarian in practice. If elders are really elders according to 1 Timothy 2:9-15, 3:1-7 and Titus 1:5-9, then they are shepherds. They lead the church comprehensively. They do not only have a lengthy meeting every third Thursday or so. As vital as the shepherd is for a flock of fluffy white animals, so the elder is for his congregation.

This means that we do not have the luxury of sitting back and waiting for perfectly-formed pastors of the church to spontaneously pop up like a piece of toast. We have to train men to be elders. As noted earlier, we need to form young men to possess the seeds of the character of a shepherd. We need rich biblical preaching that will engage men and inflame their love for God's Word. We must disciple husbands so that they will lead their wives and children to know the Lord. None of this is easy. All of this will cost you. But it must be done. We must invest in the future of the church by raising up godly men.

Biblical complementarity summons us to create rich learning environments for women. Sometimes we hear people ask if we support women teaching in the local church. We smile and reply, 'If women aren't teaching in a local church, it needs to repent at once!' By this we mean that Titus 2:3-5 necessitates the teaching of younger women by older women:

> Older women likewise are to be reverent in behavior, not slanderers or slaves to much wine. They are to teach what is good, and so train the young women to love their husbands and children, to be self-controlled, pure, working at home, kind, and submissive to their own husbands, that the word of God may not be reviled.

If a church does not feature womanly discipleship and teaching, we fear that the body will dishonor Christ and fail to produce godly women. There is a deep and even desperate need for young women to learn about the faith, homemaking, childraising, and marriage. This means biblical and theological instruction geared at a doxological feminine existence. To fail to teach these things means that Scripture will 'be reviled,' which shows us the high stakes of neglecting to teach on biblical complementarity.

Complementarians desire to see women raised up to serve the church in manifold ways. We believe that a woman can be a deaconess, as this is a service role and not a teaching position. Sometimes modern evangelicals argue that complementarity restrains women. But we know that Scripture's plan for womanhood is good. Women are in no way prevented or hindered from theological study and biblical learning. Rich teaching from a variety of sources supplements and drives a woman's hunger to live a set-apart existence.

The church's preaching and teaching should train women to pursue Christ with zeal. Indeed, God has ordained the preaching in the church to build up the whole body, and so elders are called to see themselves as the chief earthly agents of the spiritual growth of all the men and women under their care. Men are appointed for this work in a unique way. Elders have the privilege—and the high call—of guarding the church's life and doctrine, even as they guard their own life and doctrine (1 Tim. 4:16). This responsibility cannot be sublet to any other group in the church. It is the sacred charge of God to the shepherds of His flock. Complementarity thus matters hugely for the care and safety of women in the flock.

Sixth, complementarity speaks a better word about sex than secularism. No part of our world has suffered more from the advance of amoralistic postmodernism than sex. No good gift of God has undergone greater revision than this. Sex in the twenty-first century is more than a physical activity; it is for many people today nothing less than a worldview, a continual pursuit, an obsession, and the very pathway which Satan uses to speed people along to a Christless eternity.

Whenever the devil undermines God's wisdom, he replaces it with a counterfeit version. Today, we commonly hear that we live in an enlightened sexual age. Men and women do not suffer from the church's burdensome moral constraints. They are free to explore their sexual identity and experience pleasure as they see fit. The very act of pursuing and having sex is itself a moral good. It allows people to find out their true desires, and finding one's true desires without threat of shame or guilt is considered liberation. You could even call it secular salvation.

In such a climate, one would think that men and women must be thriving as never before. But this is obviously not the case. Women are in fact endangered as never before. The culture watched in awe as *Fifty Shades of Grey* played out a bondage fantasy on the big screen, with a man having the freedom to do basically whatever he liked with a submissive young woman. This was presented as exciting, good, and liberating. In reality, any man who would treat a woman in such a way is a sociopath.

Our college campuses bear all the fruits of a postmodern paradise. Young men and women are encouraged by their schools to do most anything they want sexually provided both sides give mutual consent. Though few voices will speak up and say this, the advent of an amoral sexual culture on campus has coincided exactly with the rise of 'rape culture.' Even allowing for some hysteria under this rubric, it seems evident that many young men and women have zero sense of shared sexual expectations. They have been told they can do most anything they want, that sex is just a physical experience, and that they can have it early and often. Yet this same environment is rife with division, sin, and real harm.

Young men and women are not thriving today. Many are suffering terribly from these and other influences. A recent headline in *USA Today* tells us with grave clarity what this kind of ethics produces: 'Students Flood College Counseling Offices.' One out of ten students now receives regular counseling, according to the newspaper.[3] Consider also the following from the American Psychological Association:

> In the 2010 National Survey of Counseling Center Directors, respondents reported that 44 per cent of their clients had severe psychological problems, a sharp increase from 16 per cent in 2000. The most common of these disorders are depression, anxiety, suicidal ideation, alcohol abuse, eating disorders, and self-injury. In a 2010 survey of students by the American College Health Association, 45.6 per cent

3. http://www.usatoday.com/story/news/nation/2014/04/07/college-students-flood-counseling-offices/7411333/

of students surveyed reported feeling that things were hopeless and 30.7 per cent reported feeling so depressed that it was difficult to function during the past twelve months.[4]

We are not arguing that these shocking data and all 'disorders' referenced here owe only to sexual licentiousness. But the permissive climate of the secular university only aids and abets the natural tendency of the fallen human heart to simultaneously indulge in sin and be depressed by sinful actions. Today's liberated generation labors under the weight of a guilty conscience, one that no amount of hedonism will salve. We've all been indoctrinated to believe that amorality is unrestrainably fun and fulfilling. Instead, it is in the lives of many an agent of terror and dissolution.

In such times and circumstances, we must recover the clear air of biblical sex. Sex is not an isolated good. It is given to humanity as the gift of God for the covenant of marriage. God never sanctions or blesses extramarital sex. He has made sex for the enjoyment of one man and one woman united in marriage. The biblical vision of sex is grounded in complementarity (Gen. 2:25). We are not pro-sex first and pro-marriage second. We are pro-marriage first and recognize that sex is the gift of God to those called to marriage.

There is thus a plan and intention for sex. It allows for the fullest possible union of a couple, the experience of togetherness that joins together physical, emotional, and spiritual pleasure. Sex according to God's design is not only right, but doxological. It is also vital. God has ordained that humanity continue to exist through this channel; God so esteemed sex that He made it the only means by which life

4. http://www.apa.org/about/gr/education/news/2011/college-campuses.aspx.

may be created. We cannot, however much we try, reshape procreation. Only complementarity allows for it.

In all this, we see that complementarity is not one sexual option among many. It is the gift and plan of God, the only means by which we may honor the Lord in sexual terms. To recognize the vital connection between sexual complementarity and marriage is to see that God has ordered the universe so that we may simultaneously honor His design and experience true pleasure in a romantic sense. The plan of God for a man and woman united in marriage calls us out of amoral hedonism. It speaks a better word than a sexually licentious culture. It drives men to faithfulness to one wife in pursuit of sexual delight with one woman, and it protects women by ushering them into a covenant with one man, a man totally committed to them and focused on them.

Christians do not feel embarrassed about complementarity and sexual union. We feel pity for our lost neighbors, who think that in rejecting God's plan they will find true happiness. Sex is not ultimately fulfilling, and it is not anything we want to make it. It is the gift of God, and it is given with a specific framework in mind, one that creates happiness between husband and wife, creates bonds between parents and children, and that on a much greater level images the spiritual bond between Christ and His blood-bought church. Our earthly complementarity in marriage, all aspects of it, points to the heavenly complementarity between Jesus and His people.

Seventh, complementarity helps us appreciate the goodness of God-given singleness. The church has so much to say about marriage. But this never detracts from our support of godly single men and women. Sometimes Christians wonder if those who advocate in public for the strengthening of a marriage culture view godly singles as problematic or deficient. Nothing could be further from the truth. The head of the church is a single man, Jesus Christ, who never married, had sex, or knew the joys of tousling a child's hair. He had no inside jokes with a spouse, no companion to lay beside at night, no complementary bride with whom to savor the big and small beauties of life. Yet Jesus knew God, and lived perfectly before Him. He always honored His Father. He was the happiest man who ever walked the earth, and He died with joy on His mind, even the joy of purchasing a people for Himself (Heb. 12:2).

Single men and women who seek to emulate Jesus must know that the church does not condemn them. Quite the opposite: it cheers them on as they embrace a life that Paul himself said was uniquely oriented to service in the kingdom of God (see 1 Cor. 7). Complementarians thus must make clear that we delight to promote God's vision for marriage, and will never relinquish this vision, no matter what a given society decrees. We also wish to trumpet the value of godly singleness, and to fully enfranchise the single life that is devoted to Christ and the extension of His glory. There is no tension between these two commitments, and Christians in both states must take care to support their brothers and sisters on the other side.

This, in fact, is precisely what single men and women need: they need a church. The church is not a society, organization, or club. It is a family (Rom. 12:10-13). All of us, whether married with eight children, newlywed, or single, enter the church as an orphan. Our background is in spiritual terms exactly the same: our heavenly Father adopted us as His own (Ezek. 16:1-14; Rom. 8:12-17). There is no one on this earth who was naturally born into the family of God. Every one of us came into the household of God as a desperate, lost, abandoned child. Satan, our wicked father, abandoned us, though he sought our constant destruction, and wished only for us to lose our very souls for eternity. In His infinite mercy, God has made every Christian His own child.

Single men and women may feel isolated and alone. They may experience considerable loneliness. It may be hard, abidingly hard, achingly hard, to not have a spouse and children with which one shares all the joys of this life: holidays, vacations, trips, birthdays, and the daily routines of life. But godly singles are not alone. They must not be left to themselves. They are part of the family. They are well loved by God. He is their Father. They are no different than any other saint. God has adopted them. He has abandoned their abandonment. They are His.

When God saves single men and women, He brings them into the church family. He gives them elders to watch over their souls. He calls godly men to conscionably and appropriately lend aid to single women by fixing broken faucets, scrutinizing would-be suitors, and offering counsel on tough questions. He calls godly women to conscionably and appropriately lend aid to single men by cooking them decent meals (and sending home leftovers) and welcoming them to a warm, happy home.

In these and many other ways, the church as the true family blesses single men and women. It supports them as they venture forth to glorify God in their chosen vocation. It in no ways leaves them alone to face the wilds of a sexualized, post-Christian culture. The church is the true family, and in the true family, men and women are free to use their distinctive gifts to bless the whole body. The church is not only *able* to help singles; it is *made* for unity and love, and so all who join by faith in Christ are welcome. All have a home. All have a Father.

Remember: there are no orphans in the household of God.

Conclusion

In the foregoing seven points, we have a offered a summary and synthesis of the material presented in this book. We have sought to show that complementarity owes to a master strategy, a grand design. It is far from a take-it-or-leave-it doctrine, the theological equivalent of the appendix. It is absolutely vital to making sense of our world, our faith, and our bodies.

Complementarity is less like an impediment, an obstacle to a fully realized Christianity, and much more like renewed eyesight, a gift by which people once blind to the beauty of God's plan may now behold with wonder the goodness of the created order. It is this order, this world, these bodies that Christ has claimed for His own in the here and now. It is this realm and we ourselves that Christ is now remaking for His greater renown.

This, and no other, is a design worth savoring, and a world-view worth owning.

Conclusion

The collective mind of the world boggled in July 2015 when a young American traveling to Paris stopped a terrorist attack on a speeding train, saving dozens and perhaps hundreds of lives in an instant.

Spencer Stone woke up from a nap on his way into the famed city to see a gunman, bristling with weapons, about to unload on his fellow passengers for the glory of Allah. Stone was trained in the U.S. military but had no weapons of his own to use. In a flash, he made a split-second decision to run down the aisle toward the terrorist, bear-hug him, and keep him from killing dozens, perhaps hundreds, of men and women around him. Stone did not know it, but the train attendants had fled the scene, according to reports. He was all that stood between a hail of bullets and a train of innocents.

So he ran. He tackled the gunman. He held on for dear life as the crazed man slashed him with a box-cutter, nearly cutting out his eye and almost severing his thumb. He held on while three other passengers ran to his aid and struck back at the ferocious assailant. The fight was bloody and visceral. It ended with the gunman subdued, Stone bleeding in numerous places, and a train full of passengers who had come seconds from dying. But Stone's work was not done. He had trained as a medic in the armed forces. In danger of losing consciousness, he forgot about his own wounds, and reached out to a fellow passenger bleeding profusely from the neck. His action saved a life, though it nearly cost him his own.

The Paris train attack stunned the watching world. Stone and his friends received medals for their exploits. For a brief spell, the world gaped in awe at his courage, his willingness to sacrifice himself for the good of others. Forgotten, for a brief media cycle, were exotic gender theories about the fluidity of manhood. The display of virtuous manhood seen in Stone's heroics was undeniable, even to people unaccustomed to such displays. Apparently, manhood is not dead. Apparently, there is something to calling men to be men in the biblical or traditional way.

This act of heroism reminds us of a key argument of this book. We will appreciate concepts like manhood and womanhood, complementarity, leadership and submission only when we know the grand design of God. The Lord has made us for His own glory, but He has not rendered us androgynous creatures without definitive roles. For His praise and our flourishing, He has made us male and female. Our manhood and womanhood are invested with meaning, brimming with promise, and fashioned with tenderness. He has called men to lead their families, strengthen their churches, and be forces for good in society, dying to ourselves in the image of Christ. He has called women to embrace submission in the context of the home and church, given them the valuable identity of helper, and offered them the chance to bear and nurture life.

The Lord has spoken a better word than the culture. His plan for sexuality does not involve gratifying our lusts and taking them as our identity. Sexuality is filtered in the biblical mind through complementarity. Marriage is the one and only context for sexual gratification. To fall into any other pattern is to fall prey to paganism. God does not want us to live like the animals. He wants mankind to image His holiness, intelligence, and beauty. He wants us to flourish and thrive. Because of this, He has given us certain roles to play in life. His call to conformity is no burden, no heavy weight on our shoulders that we bear with a sigh. It is a release into fields of blessing, a call to an easy yoke and a full heart.

Complementarity, we have sought to show, is given us for our good. It is like all the Scripture in this regard. As we have argued throughout, nothing the Bible teaches is unimportant. It is all true, and in its truthfulness, it is all good, and good for us. Think of what the apostle Paul says about mental and spiritual transformation: 'Do not be conformed to this world, but be transformed by the renewal of your mind, that by testing you may discern what is the will of God, what is good and acceptable and perfect' (Rom. 12:2). The upward call of the Christian is always to seek to understand Scripture. But understanding is not an end unto itself. Paul wants us to know this. He bids us come and learn not for the sake of acquiring knowledge-badges to pin on our clothes, but to be transformed such that we become wise and thus live the fullness of our lives for the glory of Christ.

We teach the whole counsel of God, from the texts that speak of ultimate things all the way to the texts that relate to the details of our existence. The words of Christ still speak, and still guard from a doctrinally weakened Christianity:

> …whoever relaxes one of the least of these commandments and teaches others to do the same will be called least in the kingdom of heaven, but whoever does them and teaches them will be called great in the kingdom of heaven (Matt. 5:19).

How striking these words are to modern ears. Jesus upholds and celebrates the teaching of God's Word—all of it.

Our Savior is not merely offering a summary judgment on Scripture, though. He is showing us how to think about the Bible. We can boil down His viewpoint to this: according to Christ, all that the Word of God teaches is true. Because all Scripture is true, all Scripture is good. One key passage for this worldview is Psalm 19:7-9, which extols the excellence of God's law:

> *The law of the LORD is perfect,*
> *reviving the soul;*
> *the testimony of the LORD is sure,*
> *making wise the simple;*
> *the precepts of the LORD are right,*
> *rejoicing the heart;*
> *the commandment of the LORD is pure,*
> *enlightening the eyes;*
> *the fear of the LORD is clean,*
> *enduring forever;*
> *the rules of the LORD are true,*
> *and righteous altogether.*

The praise given to God for His law in these verses takes us aback. As seen here and in other biblical texts, the Bible itself calls for us to worship God for the beauty and perfection and wisdom and purity and truthfulness of His Word. Our fundamental confession is this: The Bible is true. The Bible is good. The Bible's teaching is good *for us*—all of it.

All this is instructive for our understanding of complementarity. As you've seen in the preceding six chapters, we believe that if the Bible teaches a doctrine, then we must receive it and live it out with abandon. We want to be gluttons for spiritual maturity and theological understanding. We do not—or should not—crave a secular culture. We should not hunger most for the things of this world. We can enjoy God's common grace gifts, but as believers our chief delight is God Himself. We want to be like God. We want to submit ourselves to Scripture, to relentlessly seek to bring all our lives into conformity with Christ's Word so that we experience the joy of the God-focused life. We want to be *living doxology*.

The great news is that the good news takes us who are bad news and makes us new. The gospel of Christ crucified for our justification and raised for our vindication ruins us and remakes us. It takes the androgynous and makes them full-throated men and women. It takes the fatherless, those who feel cursed and alone, and gives them a Father who will never fail. The gospel takes broken marriages, unions that are being tossed around like ships in a storm at sea, riven by bitterness and cyclical, never-resolved fights, and turns them into calm, gentle streams. It takes timid, passive dads and makes them Christlike leaders of their wives and children. It takes women indoctrinated by feminism and allows them to behold the beauty of submission and service. It calls men to lead others as men and women to serve others as women. All this the gospel does and more.

Knowing and celebrating these things honors God in the extreme. This is its own reward. But let us not be misinformed. In owning these teachings and many others we've covered in this book, we recognize that we're walking into the headwind of culture. We'll face opposition for holding these views and embracing these practices. We won't get bonus points from many of our non-Christian friends and neighbors. Pastors who seize on these glorious realities may lose support and even contributions to the church. Evangelical friends may wonder why we're focusing on doctrinal matters that seem divisive. We may hear that we're the reason for disunity. *If you would just stop emphasizing complementarian teaching,* friends might say, *we could get past the difficult stuff and focus on the really important teaching of the Bible.*

We can surely love friends who do not hold our views. We can be honest about our failings and make clear that no person, church, or movement is perfect. We all must regularly confess and repent of our shortcomings. Complementarians are by no means exempt from this rhythm of grace. Where we hear of failures on our part, we are called to own these failings and turn away from them.

We should also graciously, warmly, and with the full weight of conviction seek to open their eyes to the grand design of God (per Gal. 6:1). But we also proclaim this truth: complementarity does not get in the way of the gospel. These realities are not like people jockeying for position on an airplane, one getting in the way of the other, both wishing the other would go away. The gospel creates a passion for and understanding of complementarity. You cannot divorce the two; you cannot separate one from the other. If you are to love the gospel, you cannot help but love the Christ-shaped vision of manhood and womanhood that the gospel creates. The two are one.

Many people today hold to complementarian theology. In our work at the Council on Biblical Manhood & Womanhood, we see this and rejoice in it. But we do have a burden to help the church act on its theology. If we set the mark right where Scripture has it, we don't have to worry about being seen as anti-woman and thus couch our complementarianism in a defensive posture. If we give in to cultural pressure, after all, we'll simply end up looking anxious and insecure. This isn't what God wants for His people.

We feel great compassion for those who are tasting the sting of holding to biblical truth in a fallen world. We want them to know the happiness that comes from trusting God and affirming His Word as not simply true, but good. We ourselves have seen by God's sheer grace, and His grace alone, that the Scripture has something better for us than anxiety over contested biblical teaching. God wants us to hold our ground. He wants us to stand firm in the truth (2 Tim. 1). He wants us to stand down the devil and let the world do its worst, never wavering, never losing the smile on our face that stems from His efficacious love.

The heroes of the Paris train attack are sinners like every one of us. We do not know their hearts or destinies. But we do know this: we see in Spencer Stone and his peers great courage. We want that for ourselves. But we do not, at the end of the day, only wish to hold our ground. We want to reach out in love to a world caught in lies. We want to help those around us see the beauty of manhood and womanhood, the glory of complementarity. We want them to come alive to their God-given sex and God-given roles.

As the city of God crumbles, we as members of the city of God cannot stay seated. When so many around us are struggling and in eternal peril, we must rise, and go to those trapped in sin. We must seek to rescue them. Our lives may be required of us in this grand pursuit. The cost of loving and proclaiming the truth may be great. But we must go. We have seen the grand design, and it impels us to go, preach, and celebrate the glory of God in the world of men.

Acknowledgements:

We are grateful beyond words for our beloved and excellent wives, Bethany and Amanda, who more than any others have helped us savor God's grand design for manhood and womanhood.

For our co-laborers at Midwestern Seminary and Calvary Grace, led by President Jason Allen and pastor Clint Humfrey, we are deeply thankful.

We so appreciate the staff of CBMW, including Grant Castleberry, Scott Corbin, Greg Gibson, Colin Smothers, Brittany Lind, Matt Damico, Courtney Reissig, JBMW editor Jason Duesing, Matthew Sims, Jeremy Kimble, Candi Finch, Jessi Corbin. This excellent team works very hard to provide resources to help God's people treasure biblical manhood and womanhood.

Our profound gratitude also to the CBMW board, led by Erik Thoennes, which includes Wayne Grudem, J. Ligon Duncan III, Daniel Akin, Thomas White, Jason Duesing, Jeff Purswell, and Miguel Núñez.

We very much appreciate Willie Mackenzie and the excellent team at Christian Focus Publications. It was a pleasure to work with them, and their concern for the health of God's global church is heartening. May this book find an audience all over the world by the kindness of divine providence.

To the God who does all things well, we give thanks.

THE COUNCIL ON BIBLICAL
MANHOOD AND WOMANHOOD

In 1987, CBMW was founded by a group of Christian leaders that included John Piper and Wayne Grudem. CBMW was grounded in the Danvers Statement (1988), which outlines the core commitments of the complementarian movement.

The organization was established primarily to help the church defend against the accommodation of secular feminism. At the same time, some evangelicals were beginning to experiment with an ideology that would later become known as evangelical feminism. This was a significant departure from what the church had practiced from its beginning regarding the role of men and women in the home and local church. As evangelical feminism seeks to spread, the evangelical community needs to be aware that this debate reaches ultimately to the heart of Christ's gospel and the very character of God.

The mission of The Council on Biblical Manhood and Womanhood is to set forth with joyful passion the teachings of the Bible about the complementary differences between men and women, created equally in the image of God. These teachings are essential for obedience to Scripture and for the health of the family, the church, and the broader society.

CBMW presents this good, true, and beautiful vision at its website, cbmw.org, and through the long-standing Journal for Biblical Manhood & Womanhood.

Christian Focus Publications

Our mission statement –

STAYING FAITHFUL

In dependence upon God we seek to impact the world through literature faithful to His infallible Word, the Bible. Our aim is to ensure that the Lord Jesus Christ is presented as the only hope to obtain forgiveness of sin, live a useful life and look forward to heaven with Him.

Our books are published in four imprints:

CHRISTIAN FOCUS

Popular works including biographies, commentaries, basic doctrine and Christian living.

CHRISTIAN HERITAGE

Books representing some of the best material from the rich heritage of the church.

MENTOR

Books written at a level suitable for Bible College and seminary students, pastors, and other serious readers. The imprint includes commentaries, doctrinal studies, examination of current issues and church history.

CF4•K

Children's books for quality Bible teaching and for all age groups: Sunday school curriculum, puzzle and activity books; personal and family devotional titles, biographies and inspirational stories – because you are never too young to know Jesus!

Christian Focus Publications Ltd,
Geanies House, Fearn, Ross-shire,
IV20 1TW, Scotland, United Kingdom.
www.christianfocus.com
blog.christianfocus.com